RES GESTAE DIVI AUGUSTI

THE ACHIEVEMENTS OF
THE DIVINE AUGUSTUS

with an introduction and commentary by

P. A. BRUNT

and

J. M. MOORE

OXFORD UNIVERSITY PRESS

OXFORD
UNIVERSITY PRESS

Great Clarendon Street, Oxford OX2 6DP

Oxford University Press is a department of the University of Oxford.
It furthers the University's objective of excellence in research, scholarship,
and education by publishing worldwide in

Oxford New York

Auckland Cape Town Dar es Salaam Hong Kong Karachi
Kuala Lumpur Madrid Melbourne Mexico City Nairobi
New Delhi Shanghai Taipei Toronto

With offices in

Argentina Austria Brazil Chile Czech Republic France Greece
Guatemala Hungary Italy Japan South Korea Poland Portugal
Singapore Switzerland Thailand Turkey Ukraine Vietnam

Oxford is a registered trade mark of Oxford University Press
in the UK and in certain other countries

Published in the United States
by Oxford University Press Inc., New York

© Oxford University Press 1967

First published 1967

ISBN 0–19–831772–7

25 27 29 30 28 26 24

Printed in Great Britain
on acid-free paper by
Biddles Ltd.
King's Lynn, Norfolk

PREFACE

THIS edition of the *Res Gestae* is designed for use as an historical source by sixth form pupils and undergraduates who may be studying either history or classics, some of whom may have little or no Latin or Greek. The Latin text is, therefore, accompanied by a translation, and all Latin or Greek in the notes is also translated. Some Latin words, which have no adequate English equivalents, have been left in the translation, but they are all explained in the notes or in the appendix on Roman constitutional terms.

The Latin text printed is that of V. Ehrenberg and A. H. M. Jones (*Documents Illustrating the Reigns of Augustus and Tiberius*, Clarendon Press, 1955), with minor changes of punctuation. In order to facilitate reading we have omitted the square brackets which indicate restorations of the Latin; the sense, if not the exact words, is certain, and we feel that a forest of brackets is forbidding to the readers we have in view. We have also not given the Greek paraphrase of the Latin, on which such restorations may be based, though we have occasionally referred to it in notes; it is easily accessible in Ehrenberg and Jones. Those who wish to study textual problems may turn to *Res Gestae Divi Augusti*, edited by Jean Gagé (second edition, Paris, 1950), which gives, by variations of typeface, exact indications of the authority behind each word or letter.

In the notes we have not restricted ourselves to the minimum information necessary to the understanding of what Augustus wrote, but have also tried to point out where he is tendentious, and what his purpose may have been in including or omitting certain information. We have commented fairly freely on statements which are themselves evidence of the first importance for the matters to which they relate; we have not, however, described in detail events to which Augustus merely alludes and which are more fully known from other sources, but have been content to cite standard works in English (see list of abbreviations); for instance, a commentary on the *Res Gestae* is no place for a continuous and detailed exposition of Augustus' wars. On the other hand, we found that it made for clarity to give in the introduction a brief outline of his various constitutional experiments; this is not intended to replace the fuller discussion necessary in an historical textbook, but to provide background information needed for consideration of the *Res Gestae*. Some common constitutional terms are also explained in an appendix.

We have used extensively the edition of Gagé in preparing our commentary, and the extent of our debt to it will be clear. We have also referred to the editions of E. G. Hardy (*Monumentum Ancyranum*, Oxford, 1923) and of H. Volkmann (*Res Gestae Divi Augusti*, Berlin, 1957), as well as to Mommsen's second edition (Berlin, 1883).

Since the first impression we have made in successive reprints some corrections and modifications, notably on pp. 12–14, 57, 67–8 and 84, and inserted a few Addenda which could not conveniently be introduced into the original text.

P.A.B.
J.M.M.

1973

CONTENTS

Abbreviations

CAH	*The Cambridge Ancient History*
CR	*The Classical Review*
EJ	V. Ehrenberg and A. H. M. Jones, *Documents illustrating the Reigns of Augustus and Tiberius*
Gagé	*Res Gestae Divi Augusti*, texte établi et commenté par J. Gagé (2nd ed.)
ILS	*Inscriptiones Latinae Selectae* ed. H. Dessau
Jones	A. H. M. Jones, *Studies in Roman Government and Law*
JRS	*The Journal of Roman Studies*
OCD	*The Oxford Classical Dictionary*
RG	The *Res Gestae* of Augustus
Rice Holmes	T. Rice Holmes, *Architect of the Roman Empire*
Syme	R. Syme, *The Roman Revolution*
Numbers	without other specification, e.g. '(23,1)' refer to chapters and sections in the *Res Gestae*.

INTRODUCTION

WHEN Augustus died on 19 August, AD 14, he left behind him four documents, entrusted to the Vestal Virgins for safe keeping; these documents as listed by Suetonius (*Aug.* 101, 4) were: his will; instructions for his funeral; 'a catalogue of his achievements which he wished to be inscribed on bronze tablets and set up in front of his mausoleum'; and a summary of the military and financial state of the whole empire. The catalogue of his achievements (*indicem rerum a se gestarum*) has survived, and is normally referred to as the *Res Gestae* of Augustus. Gagé (p. 9) argues that the title of the original would have been similar to that of the surviving inscription, and suggests: *Res Gestae divi Augusti, quibus orbem terrarum imperio populi Romani subiecit, et impensae quas in rem publicam populumque Romanum fecit*; 'The achievements of the divine Augustus, by which he brought the world under the empire of the Roman people, and the expenses which he bore for the state and the people of Rome'. This expresses clearly his purpose in producing the document.

The Inscription

We have three sources for this document, all from Galatia. The main one, which has been known with varying degrees of accuracy since the sixteenth century, is the *Monumentum Ancyranum*, an inscription in the temple of 'Rome and Augustus' at Ancyra in Galatia, the modern Ankara; here were inscribed on the walls of the temple the Latin text and a Greek paraphrase of it. Augustus was himself chary of the practice of the worship of sovereigns which had long been customary in Greek-speaking lands, but he permitted the erection of temples to 'Rome and Augustus', to the presiding spirit of the Roman empire coupled with his own name, and there could be no more appropriate place in which to inscribe a copy of his own account of what he had done for the Roman empire. Both the Latin and Greek texts at Ancyra are damaged, but the other two sources of the text enable a great proportion of the damaged or missing sections to be restored with a considerable measure of confidence. These two other sources are the fragments of the Greek text discovered at Apollonia in Pisidia, and the fragments of the Latin text which have been discovered at Antioch in the same district. There are no manuscript sources for the text of this document, though it is clear that Suetonius, and probably other Roman historians, consulted either the original or a copy in the Imperial archives in Rome.

Despite very minor variations of the text preserved in our three sources, it is clear that all three spring from a common original, and for the Latin version there is no reason to doubt the claim of the first sentence of the work that it is a copy of the inscription set up in Rome on the express instructions of Augustus, with the minor reservation that the Appendix is presumably an addition made for provincial readers; the Preface has similarly been modified for the same audience. The Greek version is not faithful enough to be called a translation, but it is a fairly close paraphrase. It is clear that both the Greek versions spring from the same original, and that that original was translated from the text of the Latin version more or less as we have it to-day; thus the Greek version permits the restoration of defective passages in the Latin. Where the Latin text is restored in this way, the actual words may be uncertain, but the sense is not in doubt.

Once the decision had been taken to 'publish' the work in Galatia, it would have been necessary to have a Greek version as well as the original Latin; the Latin version would have been set up in the most important towns, like Ancyra, and in places with a large Latin-speaking population, like Antioch which had a colony of Romans, but Greek was the common literary language of the Near East, and it would have been necessary to provide a Greek translation for the majority of local readers. It may have been prepared in Rome on Augustus' own instructions, but in view of its inaccuracies, it is far more likely that it was produced locally.[1]

The Literary Genre

At funerals of great men at Rome it was the practice for some member of the family to deliver an oration commemorating the dead man's virtues and achievements. Often men left behind them

[1] On the origin of the Greek version see Gagé; 9ff., and references cited there.

more permanent memorials in the form of inscriptions recording their careers and deeds. The earliest of such *elogia* belongs to a consul of 298 BC. Augustus himself set up retrospective *elogia* of Rome's great men in his new forum. One such inscription recorded the career of Marius (*ILS* 59): 'Gaius Marius, son of Gaius, consul seven times, praetor, tribune of the plebs, quaestor, augur, tribune of the soldiers. He was specially appointed to wage war with Jugurtha, king of the Numidians, whom he captured and at his triumph in his second consulship ordered to be led before his chariot. He was elected consul for the third time in his absence. In his fourth consulship he destroyed the army of the Teutones. In his fifth he routed the Cimbri, and triumphed a second time over them and the Teutones. He freed the republic, when consul a sixth time, from the rising of a tribune of the plebs and a praetor, who had taken up arms and had seized the Capitol. When over seventy, he was expelled from his fatherland in civil war and restored by arms, and became consul a seventh time. From his war-spoils taken from the Cimbri and Teutones he built, as the victor, a temple to Honour and Valour. In triumphal garb and patrician boots he entered the senate. ...' The *Res Gestae* may be regarded as a development out of such *elogia*, more elaborate indeed, just as Augustus' achievements were more grandiose.

These *elogia* would hardly contain any directly untrue claims, since there would be too many people who could disprove them. This imposed limitations on an author who wished to represent his actions in the best possible light for posterity. However, the account of achievements might be highly selective. Thus a historian may rely with reasonable certainty on statements of fact, though he must regard with reserve any statement which includes interpretation of facts. What is omitted in such an account may be as informative as what is stated, since it will indicate the way in which the author wished to 'slant' his narrative. For example, in the *Res Gestae* Augustus' opponents do not appear by name; Antony is a 'faction', Brutus and Cassius are enemies of Rome, and it is implied that Sextus Pompeius is a pirate.

Augustus' Res Gestae

Augustus addresses the text of the *Res Gestae* to Roman citizens, and especially to the inhabitants of Rome itself; this may be seen from a number of points, such as the fact that he only mentions the provinces where he is recording their recovery or conquest for the Roman people,[1] and the way in which virtually all the *impensae* (expenditure) mentioned refer to Rome. He omits many acts of financial generosity to Italian or provincial cities, and, by contrast, details of his largesses to the Roman plebs and of the various games he gave can hardly have been of any interest to provincials. It is natural that he should have written in this way since the *Res Gestae* was designed to be inscribed at Rome.

Therefore it is clear that, although all our surviving sources of the document come from Galatia, this is Augustus' statement of his achievements, composed for the people of Rome. It is equally clear that such a document was bound to be an apologia, containing the things which Augustus wished to be remembered about his life, and omitting things which were inconsistent with the picture he was drawing. Through the whole document he balances honours and position in the state with his achievements and the expenses he undertook in the public interest; the expenses listed are those undertaken with money which was inherited, obtained from spoils of war or drawn from his private fortune; he does not include public expenditure undertaken under his guidance. Always it is the first person that is stressed, and it is Augustus' own actions that are considered.

The nature of Augustus' position has led some to compare the *Res Gestae* with the great royal inscriptions of the East such as that of Darius at Behistun, but this is not a sound parallel. In some passages in the *Res Gestae* the royal flavour almost appears, as for example where Augustus lists the kings who fled to him for refuge (32), or the honours he received, in particular the vows made and fulfilled for his safety (9; 11–12); on the other hand, much is routine, and in places very monotonous, detail of expenditure. The overall impression resembles that of the Roman *elogia* referred to above.

Not only does the document omit those things which Augustus probably wished forgotten, but it is also not a complete enumeration of his achievements: it only alludes to part of his legislation, leaves out his administrative reforms, and does not fully cover his revival of the old Roman religion. Although some events in the field of foreign affairs are mentioned, there is no explanation of the policy in-

[1] For an apparent exception, see 24,1 and note.

volved. Augustus is not concerned to commemorate the achievements of the senate and people of Rome at a time when in strict constitutional form he was only the leading man, but to enumerate those for which he was administratively responsible.

Although the *Res Gestae* does not offer a comprehensive survey and justification of Augustus' policy and position as a whole, it is designed to demonstrate and justify the unique position of pre-eminence which he had come to hold. After a brief introduction describing his entry into public life, he deals rapidly with his triumphs and military successes; this precedes and implicitly justifies the unparalleled accumulation of honours bestowed on him.[1] In listing these honours he more than once stresses that they were bestowed by the people as well as the senate, and emphasizes that he was unwilling to accept untraditional, i.e. unrepublican, honours or powers. This plea is an example of clever propaganda writing; it may be true that he accepted no individual office or position for which no Republican precedent whatever could be found, questionable though some of the precedents were, but he naturally did not mention that there was no precedent for any one man holding so many different positions and powers at the same time. He then passes to the least controversial section of the *Res Gestae* (14–33), in which he lists his expenditure and those successes of war and foreign policy which he particularly wished to be commemorated, and which could properly be ascribed to his own efforts. With his claim to glory in this field it would have been difficult for anyone to quarrel, and it leads up well to the last two chapters.

Chapter 34 deals in simple terms with the equation that great achievements merit great honours, though this is not explicitly stated: Augustus had extinguished the Civil Wars and restored constitutional government; therefore he received exceptional honours, which are properly recorded in a document such as this; the result of these honours is pre-eminence in *auctoritas*, 'influence', which, it is implied, is fully justified. Chapter 35 tells how he received from the senate and people the title *Pater Patriae*, 'Father of his Country'. The full implications of both these chapters will be dealt with in the relevant notes; suffice it here to say that the official title was the highest honour that could be bestowed on a Roman. We have a fitting climax to the work.

[1] Compare the suggestion above that there is an element of accounting in the *Res Gestae*, honours balanced by achievements.

Date and Composition

The *Res Gestae* was one of three documents which Augustus deposited with the Vestal Virgins, along with his will, in April, AD 13 (Suet., *Aug.* 101). It is evident that it was touched up after his death by Tiberius; in 8,4 there is a reference to the census of AD 14, and the last sentence is dated after 23 September, AD 13. However, in the main the document had reached its final form much earlier than AD 13. Passages in which numbers are given for Augustus' years of tribunician power or the like were brought up to date (4,2; 4,4; 22; 35,2), but there are few allusions to events after 2 BC.[1] The title of 'Father of his Country', which Augustus received in that year, makes a climax to the whole work. But, if the document, as we have it, represents a draft of 2 BC, it is still unlikely that this was the first. Augustus had probably completed the great mausoleum on which his memorial was to be inscribed in 28 BC (Suet., *Aug.* 100), and by 28/7 he already had much to record; he had saved Rome from oriental tyranny and restored the Republic, according to the official view, and earned his unique name by his services to the state. He was certainly anxious about his reputation with posterity; he wrote an autobiography which went down to the Cantabrian war of 26/5 BC (*ibid.* 85). His health was delicate; in 23 BC he nearly died, and he is unlikely to have had no *elogium* ready even at this early date. It seems probable, indeed, that the famous statement in 34,3 belongs to a draft of this time, and that it was not discarded later, though it was not very apposite to Augustus' position after he ceased to hold the consulship regularly (see note *ad loc.*). Many attempts have been made to uncover different 'layers' in the final text, but it is beyond the scope of this introduction to review these speculative theories.[2]

Style

Augustus' views on style were known in the ancient world, and Suetonius and others preserve a number of passages from his writings. He favoured clarity rather than the ornate 'Asiatic' style, and did not hesitate to use prepositions with the names of towns or to

[1] 6,2 (AD 4 and 13); 8,4 (AD 14); 14,1 (AD 2 and 4); 17 (AD 6); 20,3 (AD 12); 22,1 (AD 6); 27,2 (AD 2–?6); 30,1 (AD 4); 33 (AD 4–5).

[2] For a discussion see Gagé, pp. 16ff. Cf. also 26,2 n.

repeat conjunctions, in order to make his meaning clear (Suet., *Aug.*
86). Aulus Gellius comments on these qualities in the following
terms (*Noctes Atticae* XV, 7, 3): 'I was led on by the elegance of the
style, which was neither morose nor tense, but easy and simple . . .';
he goes on to quote a letter from Augustus to his grandson Gaius.
The style of the *Res Gestae* displays just these qualities. There is
none of the bombastic boastfulness which may be seen in some
funerary monuments; rather, Augustus has left a cool record of fact
which is on occasion dry to the point of tedium, as in his list of
expenditure. There is a touch of pomposity in the stress on 'I' which
runs through the work, and there is no reticence about the peculiar
honours which he had received and, as he makes clear, felt he had
deserved. This trait emerges elsewhere: in a simple letter to Tiberius about a gambling session he describes his generosity during the
game, and ends: *benignitas enim mea me ad caelestem gloriam efferet*,
'my liberality will bring me the glory of a god' (Suet., *Aug.* 71, 3).
This is hardly the remark of a man who was habitually modest (no
doubt he liked Horace telling him (*Odes* III, 3, 11) that he would
recline amongst the gods drinking nectar). On the other hand, the
nature of the *Res Gestae* is such that a certain self-glorification is
proper, and Augustus keeps it within reasonable limits. The elegance and effectiveness of the style may perhaps best be seen in the
last two chapters (34–5), where the peroration shows delicate
fluency and admirable economy, while at the same time it gives a
strong and effective finish to the whole work.

A Note on Sources

The sources for Augustus' life and reign are on the whole poor.
Cicero's letters and *Philippics* provide abundant information for
March 44–summer 43. There is a very detailed and generally reliable account of events down to 36 in Appian's *Civil Wars*, written
in the second century AD, but probably based on the contemporary
history of C. Asinius Pollio (consul 40), a former friend of Antony
who lived in honourable retirement in Augustus' reign but ab-
stained from flattery of the victor. Plutarch's lives of Brutus and
Antony are valuable for the triumviral period. The history of
Cassius Dio is preserved complete for the years down to 10 BC, and
in large part for the rest of Augustus' life. A Bithynian by birth, he
had a distinguished senatorial career at Rome *c.* AD 190–229. He

was not uncritical, but his sources are unknown, and he himself complains that it was hard to find out the truth about events after 27 BC. He also tends to refer practices of the later Principate back into the time of Augustus. Still, with all its faults, his history is the main narrative source from 36 onwards. Velleius is useful chiefly on wars, of some of which he was an eye-witness; he is adulatory of Augustus and still more of Tiberius, in whose reign he wrote his brief history. Suetonius aimed in his lives of the Caesars at portraying their characters rather than at analysing their policy or at narrating events; his order is not chronological, and important matters are lightly treated or omitted altogether; but he has many interesting anecdotes and quotes verbatim from Augustus' writings in his lives of Augustus, Tiberius and Claudius. Livy and the Augustan poets provide valuable evidence of what some contemporaries thought; how far their opinions were representative is a question which can never be settled. We need not assume that any of them wrote only what he thought would please Augustus, or that they were all insincere in expressing sentiments which must have given him pleasure. There are, of course, scattered allusions to Augustus' life and reign in many other later writers, notably in the works of Tacitus, whose *Annals* begin with a *résumé* of Augustus' achievements and of the varying judgements men passed on them. Much important material is to be found in inscriptions and papyri; see for a selection V. Ehrenberg and A. H. M. Jones, *Documents illustrating the reigns of Augustus and Tiberius*. Of all such documents the *Res Gestae* is far the most precious, not only for the light it casts on Augustus himself but for many statements of facts, for which it is the only or most reliable evidence.

The Constitutional Position of Augustus

The following brief sketch of what may be termed the various constitutional experiments of Augustus is confined to his position in and after 27 BC; he had relied on the triumviral power from November 43 at least until the term fixed by law had expired, probably at the end of 33, and he held the consulship continuously from 31 to 27, was backed by the 'oath of allegiance' and the general support of the West against Antony, and also may have continued to use some of the powers of a triumvir: on this period see notes on 1; 7,1; 25,2; 34,1.

Augustus claims that in his sixth and seventh consulships (28/7 BC) he transferred the Republic from his power to the control of the senate and people of Rome (34,1). The restoration of the Republic was widely referred to by writers of the Augustan age: Ovid (*Fasti*, I, 589) refers to the anniversary of the day when 'every province was given back to our people', and Velleius says (II, 89): 'In the twentieth year civil wars were brought to an end, foreign wars buried, peace recalled; the frenzy of arms was everywhere lulled to sleep, the laws recovered their vigour, the courts their authority, the senate its majesty, the *imperium* of the magistrates was restored to its ancient extent, . . . the pristine form of the republic was recalled as of old'. By contrast with these near contemporary and perhaps partly 'inspired' views, Dio dates the autocracy from this moment (LII, 1, 1; LIII, 11, 4). Tacitus everywhere implies that Augustus' position was monarchical.

There is truth in both views, yet Dio and Tacitus hit the reality more exactly. In 27 Augustus did lay down extraordinary, dictatorial powers; but he received for ten years a huge province, consisting of Syria, Cilicia, Cyprus, Gaul and Spain (with the possible exception of Baetica), together with Egypt which he administered virtually as a private estate (27,1 n.). He took these provinces on the ground that they were most liable to invasion or internal revolt, and promised to restore them to the senate even before the ten years were up, if it proved safe to do so. In fact, his tenure was renewed from 18 BC at intervals of five or ten years, and though he surrendered Cyprus and Gallia Narbonensis in 22, and Baetica, if it was ever his, he was to receive compensation elsewhere (see below). From the first, most of the army was in his provinces, though there were legions in Africa, Illyricum and Macedonia, how many we do not know. He could govern his provinces as consul, as he did until 23; it may not have been pre-arranged that he should hold the consulship each year, but of course he was undefeatable whenever he chose to stand. When and if he ceased to be consul, he could retain his provinces as proconsul for the rest of his term; this was what happened in 23. As consul, he had *imperium* in Rome and Italy, and seems to have claimed a right to override proconsuls in provinces not committed to his own charge (24,1 n. and p. 81). Moreover the oath of allegiance bound all subjects of Rome to him (25,2 n.). His enormous *auctoritas* ensured that on all issues his views would be accepted (pp. 84f and 34,3 n.). His honours, especially the name of

Augustus, symbolized both the gratitude felt towards him as the saviour of the state and the pre-eminence of his position.

Thus there had been a return to legality, and Augustus exercised in strict law only a special commission for a fixed period, entrusted to him by senate and people. Precedents could be invoked on his behalf; Marius had been consul continuously from 104 to 100, and Pompey had been consul while governing Spain through legates. But these precedents were themselves abnormal, and taken as a whole Augustus' true position certainly infringed Cicero's principle that no single man should have more power than the whole Republic. From 27 to 24 he was abroad, and this may have made his dominance less apparent. But his monopoly of the consulship each year denied to others access to what still nominally counted as the highest office of state. A serious conspiracy, led by Murena, perhaps the consul in 23, and by Fannius Caepio is usually dated to 23 (Dio puts it in 22); this may have prompted Augustus to reconsider his settlement of 27 and to secure his power less obtrusively. In 23 he was also seriously ill, and he may have tired of performing the routine duties of a consul. At any rate, in July he resigned, and received other rights in return. This constitutes the second constitutional settlement, for which see Dio LIII, 32.

From this moment Augustus dates the years of his 'reign' by his tenure of the tribunician power (*tribunicia potestas*). It is not clear when Augustus actually received the tribunician power: The date given by Appian (*BC* V, 132) and Orosius (VI, 18, 34) is 36; Dio (XLIX, 15, 6) says that he then received only tribunician inviolability, while the full power was granted for life in 30 (LI, 19, 6) – but also in 23 (LIII, 32, 5)! These discrepancies have been explained in various ways. It can easily be supposed that Appian and Orosius confused the grant of inviolability, a privilege of the tribunes, with the grant of the tribunician power. It has been held that in 30 Augustus was merely offered and did not take the tribunician power, or that he took it and surrendered it in 27, only to receive it again in 23, or that Dio has confused the full tribunician power with one of its ingredients, the *ius auxilii*, (pp. 11f) probably granted in an extended form in that, whereas tribunes could exercise it only in the city of Rome, the emperors could exercise it throughout the empire. If, on the other hand, the full tribunician power was conferred on Augustus as early as 30, probably with the extension described above, then in 23 his tenure became 'annual and perpetual', and he was given the right to count the years for which he held it, beginning in 23. This is what he did do, and it shows at least that the tribunician power only assumed importance for him at that time; the chronological puzzle outlined above is of no great importance.

The tribunician power Augustus received may be analysed briefly as follows. First, he received the right to submit legislative 'bills' to the people, and to summon the senate, and put motions in that body also. He did on occasion use the former right (cf. 6,2), but very often his *auctoritas* was such that he could get others to propose what he wished to see enacted, as in the case of the Lex Papia Poppaea, where the consuls of AD 9 sponsored a measure emending the marriage law which Augustus had passed in 18 BC through his tribunician power. Thus Augustus received some compensation for losing the similar powers of the consul. However, motions were considered in the senate in the order of seniority of the magistracy held by the proposer; the seniority of a tribune was very low, and thus Augustus needed and received the subsidiary right of putting the first motion at any meeting, which has been conveniently called the *ius primae relationis*.

Secondly, the tribunician power included the right to veto (*ius intercessionis*). Had the emperors chosen to use this right to the full, it would have given them a negative control over all aspects of government. There are examples quoted in our sources of later emperors using the veto,[1] but normally proposals would not be brought before the senate unless the emperor was known to approve; if they did get as far as the senate, they could usually be checked by a mere expression of opinion rather than a formal veto; cf. Tac., *Ann.* III, 52–5.

Thirdly, the tribunician power included *coercitio*, the right of every magistrate to compel reluctant citizens to obey his orders, and to inflict sanctions if necessary. This power would have been redundant for Augustus unless it is held that he was without *imperium* in Rome at any period after 23 BC (see below).

Lastly, he received the *ius auxilii*, the power to help officially citizens who were being oppressed by other magistrates. When a tribune exercised this right, he might also investigate the case (*cognitio*) to assure himself that the situation justified his intervention. It has

[1] Compare Tac., *Ann.* III, 70: Tiberius vetoes a charge of treason; Dio LX, 4, 5: Claudius vetoes the condemnation of Gaius' memory; Tac., *Ann.* XIV, 48; XVI, 11 for Nero.

been argued that the appellate jurisdiction of the emperors was in part derived from the *ius auxilii* in this way, especially as the tribunician power of the emperor was apparently active throughout the empire; this may be the truth that lies behind a confused statement in Dio LI, 19, since it appears from Suetonius (*Tib.* 11) that Tiberius used his tribunician power in Rhodes. However, the emperors exercised jurisdiction in the first instance as well as appellate jurisdiction, and it seems necessary to derive at least the former jurisdiction even in Rome and Italy from their tenure of *imperium* (cf. pp. 13f.).

When Augustus laid down his consulship, he still retained *imperium* as governor of the provinces entrusted to him; it was his tenure of these provinces which was renewed at intervals of five or ten years. The form of his *imperium* was now modified. It was now that of a proconsul, and a proconsul forfeited *imperium* if he entered the city of Rome. As it was obviously desirable that Augustus should be free to enter when he pleased, it was provided that in such circumstances he should retain his *imperium* in Rome. This *imperium* was also now made *maius*, 'greater', which meant that he could, of right, override the governors of all provinces; this clarified the rather ambiguous situation of 27–23, when his interference as consul was perhaps technically justified, but was contrary to normal practice in the late Republic.

The effect of the changes may be summarized as follows: Augustus' power in the provinces was now certainly no less than it was when he was consul, and it was made clear that he had the right to interfere whenever and wherever he wished. He had, however, lost some power at home, at least in appearance; a proconsul normally had no executive authority in Italy.[1] The grant of tribunician power made up for some of the power he had surrendered, but did not give him so much; it is truly described by Tacitus as *summi fastigii vocabulum*, 'the *title* of the highest eminence in the state'. It was a title with convenient associations, since the tribunes had always been the officers who protected the ordinary people against tyranny. The power was used by the early emperors, and it may be that before the Principate was firmly founded the rights inherent in the tribunician power may have seemed more likely to be important in practice than they turned out to be, once

[1] But see a possible alternative suggestion below.

everyone had recognized the necessity for monarchy. In fact, the tribunician power became a convenient way of numbering the years of an emperor's reign, and a useful republican cloak to be used in disguising the reality of power, which depended without question on *imperium*.

The 'second settlement' of 23 BC was followed in 22 by offers of the dictatorship to Augustus both in his absence and when he had returned to Rome, and of a consulship which was to be 'annual and perpetual'; there was further rioting in 21–19, and the people kept a consulship open for Augustus in 21 and again for 19. The common people were presumably dissatisfied because, as indicated above, Augustus had in appearance or reality lost his power of jurisdiction and executive authority at home, and was no longer entitled to have the *fasces*[1] carried in front of him in the city: he lacked at least the semblance of authority. Dio records that in 19 he was given the right to the *fasces* and to sit between the consuls (LIV, 10, 5); from that time he at least looked like a consul, and this may have satisfied the people, and could explain why there was no further agitation that he should hold the consulship. Dio, however, goes further in the same passage, and seems to assert that Augustus received consular power for life, of which the insignia were only the symbols.

Jones (chapter 1) infers that it was only from 19 that Augustus recovered consular authority in Rome and Italy itself, in virtue of which he could command troops in Italy and exercise jurisdiction there. This hypothesis is hardly needed to explain his command of troops in Italy *outside* Rome; even in the late Republic, proconsuls must have had command over troops on their way to or from provinces and the right to levy soldiers; hence they could exercise *imperium* in Italy. However, some of Augustus' praetorian guard were eventually stationed *in* the city, and he clearly required more power than a Republican proconsul both for command of these soldiers and for jurisdiction, which depended on possession of *imperium*. Further, the *insignia* could hardly have been bestowed on a man who did not enjoy the power they symbolised! His tribunician power, his supreme *auctoritas* (see pp. 84f and 34,3 n.) or *ad hoc* grants (e.g. of consular power to take the census in 8 BC and AD 14)[2]

[1] On the *fasces*, see 4,1 n.

[2] In *RG* 8, 3–4, Augustus does not say that he *took* consular *imperium* in order to hold the censuses, but only *by what power* he was entitled to hold them.

do not fully explain all his uses of *imperium*. It has also been argued that the right given him in 23 to retain *imperium* after crossing the *pomerium* (the sacred boundary of Rome) implied the right also to *use* it in Rome and Italy; on this view, in 23 Augustus lost no real power, but only the outward appearance of it; it was only the insignia which he lacked until 19, and received then (Brunt, *C.R.*, 1962, 70ff.). But it would have been unexampled to hold the *imperium* without the *insignia*. The best solution is, then, that within the *pomerium* Augustus lacked both the *imperium* and its *insignia* between 23 and 19, though elsewhere in Italy Republican precedents would have allowed him to retain both and to command troops, who could have been regarded as merely in transit to or from his provinces overseas. But the disorders that occurred in Rome in these years encouraged him to meet popular demands by acquiring both *imperium* and its *insignia* in the city itself. Thus in 19 he recovered what he had lost in 23 without the disadvantage of monopolizing one consulship year by year.

After this, the position of Augustus did not remain static for the rest of his long reign; Tacitus says that he 'gradually increased his power, and drew into his own hands the functions of the senate, the magistrates and the laws' (*Ann* I, 2). This refers in particular to encroachments on the administration of Rome and Italy. Thus senators he nominated took over the administration of Italian roads and Rome's water supply; in both cases he obtained the sanction of the senate (Dio LIV,8,4; EJ, 278), which could hardly have been withheld. Equestrian prefects of his choice became responsible for fire precautions at Rome and for provisioning the city with grain. Probably he was always careful to seek the senate's approval when thus enlarging his own responsibilities.

Augustus' power also increased in the provinces. It is true that in 22 BC he handed the peaceful provinces of Gallia Narbonensis and Cyprus back to the senate (see above), but his own power increased. All new provinces passed to the emperor; so when the frontier moved forward to the Danube, all the troops in Macedonia were moved forward out of the control of the senate. Illyricum was transferred to Augustus in 11 BC,[1] and Sardinia in AD 6. In the end only one legion, in Africa, was left under the command of a pro-consul: all other legionary armies were under commanders who had been picked by the emperor, for loyalty as well as talent. Thus, since

[1] Syme (p. 394) prefers 12 BC.

27, when the nearest large army, that of Illyricum, was still commanded by a proconsul, Augustus' military control had become more complete. It must be noted, however, that even in 27 he had a praetorian guard, 9,000 strong, to provide for his personal security, and at all times he had the means of repressing opposition by military force.

It would, however, be a mistake to represent his power as depending mainly on the support of the army. In the triumvirate he rose to power as a military leader, and as *princeps* he sought to keep the soldiers loyal by a system of rewards (see 3,3; 15,3; 16; 17,2 with notes). The mutinies of AD 14, which Tiberius was able to suppress without making any permanent concessions, show that in his later years at least Augustus had not been wholly successful in making the soldiers content, but also that the régime was strong enough to disregard their grievances. The armies were only dangerous to an emperor if they could find leaders among the ruling class, from whom the commanders and higher officers were drawn. It is significant that after the civil wars Augustus gave up his practice of addressing the troops as his 'fellow-soldiers' (Suet., *Aug.* 25). His aim was now to restore discipline in the armies and to rely rather on the consent of the whole citizen body, and particularly on that of the higher classes, senators and *equites*,[1] who were needed for the tasks of government.

In an edict he expressed the wish that 'it may be granted to me to establish the state safely and soundly in its seat and to reap from this the fruit that I seek, namely to be called the author of the best constitution and to carry with me in death the hope that the foundations of the state which I shall have laid will remain unshaken' (Suet., *Aug.* 28). For two centuries this prayer was answered. Augustus owed his success partly to the accident that he lived long. Men were habituated to the new order; how few, says Tacitus, were alive in AD 14 who had seen the Republic (*Ann.* I, 3). Still more important was his care to conciliate possible opponents. He claims to have won universal consent. No doubt this goes too far; there were a few plots, and some discontent persisted among those who dared not conspire (*Ann.* I, 10). But one man cannot govern an empire; Augustus needed the active collaboration of the class who had the experience and tradition of governing, and it is clear that he secured

---

[1] On the *equites*, see 14,2 n.

it. Caesar, who had not concealed his autocracy, was killed by men whom he had marked out for honour, some of whom had served him well in the past, but who were not prepared to be merely his ministers: Augustus was recognized as father of his country on the motion of Messalla, a noble who had once fought for Brutus and Cassius.

The constitutional arrangements made by Augustus are important as a partial explanation of his success in winning the consent of the upper classes. They gave him the necessary legal powers to perform his executive tasks, and legality in itself was important to the Roman mind. They enabled him to guide policy in general within a framework which preserved the Republican forms. The Republican constitution was hallowed by antiquity; and it was as a Republic that Rome had grown great. Even in a town so remote as Milan Brutus still had a statue in Augustus' time as 'the founder and defender of laws and liberty' (Suet., *Rhetoricians* 6). These were sentiments which he could not ignore, but which he could also accommodate more easily to his personal supremacy, because after 27 BC hardly any one alive had actually participated in the free functioning of the Republic, and the senate was more and more composed of new men, from all over Italy, who were less imbued with the tradition of the old nobility; moreover, the system after 27 did involve more freedom and more consultation with the senate than had been known since 43.

Augustus' success is, however, not merely to be accounted for in constitutional terms; his conduct of affairs in general, his munificence, his conquests and enhancing of Roman prestige abroad all contributed; and the selection of material which he made for inclusion in the *Res Gestae* shows that he himself thought that these aspects of his life were not less important for his own honour, and presumably for the stability of his régime and of the power which it was his ambition to hand down to his descendants.

RES GESTAE DIVI AUGUSTI

RERUM gestarum divi Augusti, quibus orbem terrarum imperio populi Romani subiecit, et impensarum quas in rem publicam populumque Romanum fecit, incisarum in duabus aheneis pilis, quae sunt Romae positae, exemplar subiectum.

1 Annos undeviginti natus exercitum privato consilio et privata impensa comparavi, per quem rem publicam a dominatione factionis oppressam in libertatem vindicavi. *2* Eo nomine senatus decretis honorificis in ordinem suum me adlegit, C. Pansa et A. Hirtio consulibus, consularem locum sententiae dicendae tribuens, et imperium mihi dedit. *3* Res publica ne quid detrimenti caperet, me propraetore simul cum consulibus providere iussit. *4* Populus autem eodem anno me consulem, cum cos. uterque in bello cecidisset, et triumvirum rei publicae constituendae creavit.

2 Qui parentem meum trucidaverunt, eos in exilium expuli iudiciis legitimis ultus eorum facinus, et postea bellum inferentis rei publicae vici bis acie.

3 Bella terra et mari civilia externaque toto in orbe terrarum saepe gessi, victorque omnibus veniam petentibus civibus peperci. *2* Externas gentes, quibus tuto ignosci potuit, conservare quam excidere malui. *3* Millia civium Romanorum sub sacramento meo fuerunt circiter quingenta. Ex quibus deduxi in colonias aut remisi in municipia sua stipendis emeritis millia aliquanto plura quam trecenta, et iis omnibus agros adsignavi aut pecuniam pro praemiis militiae dedi. *4* Naves cepi sescentas praeter eas, si quae minores quam triremes fuerunt.

4 Bis ovans triumphavi et tris egi curulis triumphos et appellatus sum viciens et semel imperator, decernente pluris triumphos mihi

THE ACHIEVEMENTS OF THE DIVINE AUGUSTUS

A COPY is set out below of 'The achievements of the Divine Augustus, by which he brought the world under the empire of the Roman people, and of the expenses which he bore for the state and people of Rome'; the original is engraved on two bronze pillars set up at Rome.

1 At the age of nineteen on my own responsibility and at my own BC 44
expense I raised an army, with which I successfully championed
the liberty of the republic when it was oppressed by the tyranny of
a faction. **2** On that account the senate passed decrees in my
honour enrolling me in its order in the consulship of Gaius Pansa BC 43
and Aulus Hirtius, assigning me the right to give my opinion among
the consulars and giving me *imperium*. **3** It ordered me as a
propraetor to provide in concert with the consuls that the republic
should come to no harm. **4** In the same year, when both consuls
had fallen in battle, the people appointed me consul and triumvir
for the organization of the republic.

2 I drove into exile the murderers of my father, avenging their BC 43
crime through tribunals established by law; and afterwards, when
they made war on the republic, I twice defeated them in battle. BC 42

3 I undertook many civil and foreign wars by land and sea
throughout the world, and as victor I spared the lives of all citizens
who asked for mercy. **2** When foreign peoples could safely be
pardoned I preferred to preserve rather than to exterminate them.
3 The Roman citizens who took the soldier's oath of obedience to
me numbered about 500,000. I settled rather more than 300,000 of
these in colonies or sent them back to their home towns after their
period of service; to all these I assigned lands or gave money as
rewards for their military service. **4** I captured six hundred ships,
not counting ships smaller than triremes.

4 I celebrated two ovations and three curule triumphs and I was
twenty-one times saluted as *imperator*. The senate decreed still

senatu, quibus omnibus supersedi. Laurum de fascibus deposui in
Capitolio, votis quae quoque bello nuncupaveram solutis. 2 Ob res
a me aut per legatos meos auspicis meis terra marique prospere
gestas quinquagiens et quinquiens decrevit senatus supplicandum
esse dis immortalibus. Dies autem, per quos ex senatus consulto
supplicatum est, fuere DCCCLXXXX. 3 In triumphis meis ducti
sunt ante currum meum reges aut regum liberi novem. 4 Consul
fueram terdeciens, cum scribebam haec, et eram septimum et
tricensimum tribuniciae potestatis.

5   Dictaturam et apsenti et praesenti mihi delatam et a populo et a
senatu, M. Marcello et L. Arruntio consulibus non recepi. 2 Non
sum deprecatus in summa frumenti penuria curationem annonae,
quam ita administravi, ut intra dies paucos metu et periclo praesenti
civitatem universam liberarem impensa et cura mea. 3 Consulatum quoque tum annuum et perpetuum mihi delatum non recepi.

6   Consulibus M. Vinicio et Q. Lucretio et postea P. Lentulo et Cn.
Lentulo et tertium Paullo Fabio Maximo et Q. Tuberone senatu
populoque Romano consentientibus ut curator legum et morum
summa potestate solus crearer, nullum magistratum contra morem
maiorum delatum recepi. 2 Quae tum per me geri senatus voluit,
per tribuniciam potestatem perfeci, cuius potestatis conlegam et
ipse ultro quinquiens a senatu depoposci et accepi.

7   Triumvirum rei publicae constituendae fui per continuos annos
decem. 2 Princeps senatus fui usque ad eum diem quo scripseram
haec per annos quadraginta. 3 Pontifex maximus, augur, XV
virum sacris faciundis, VII virum epulonum, frater arvalis, sodalis
Titius, fetialis fui.

8   Patriciorum numerum auxi consul quintum iussu populi et
senatus. 2 Senatum ter legi, et in consulatu sexto censum populi
conlega M. Agrippa egi. Lustrum post annum alterum et quadra-

more triumphs to me, all of which I declined. I laid the bay leaves with which my *fasces* were wreathed in the Capitol after fulfilling all the vows which I had made in each war.   2 On fifty-five occasions the senate decreed that thanksgivings should be offered to the immortal gods on account of the successes on land and sea gained by me or by my legates acting under my auspices. The days on which thanksgivings were offered in accordance with decrees of the senate numbered eight hundred and ninety.   3 In my triumphs nine kings or children of kings were led before my chariot.   4 At the time of writing I have been consul thirteen times and am in the   AD 14 thirty-seventh year of tribunician power.

5   The dictatorship was offered to me by both senate and people in my absence and when I was at Rome in the consulship of Marcus   BC 22 Marcellus and Lucius Arruntius, but I refused it.   2 I did not decline in the great dearth of corn to undertake the charge of the corn-supply, which I so administered that within a few days I delivered the whole city from apprehension and immediate danger at my own cost and by my own efforts.   3 At that time the consulship was also offered to me, to be held each year for the rest of my life, and I refused it.

6   In the consulship of Marcus Vinicius and Quintus Lucretius,   BC 19 and afterwards in that of Publius and Gnaeus Lentulus, and thirdly   BC 18 in that of Paullus Fabius Maximus and Quintus Tubero, the senate   BC 11 and people of Rome agreed that I should be appointed supervisor of laws and morals without a colleague and with supreme power, but I would not accept any office inconsistent with the custom of our ancestors.   2 The measures that the senate then desired me to take I carried out in virtue of my tribunician power. On five occasions, of my own initiative, I asked for and received from the senate a colleague in that power.

7   I was triumvir for the organization of the republic for ten consecutive years.   2 Up to the day of writing I have been *princeps senatus* for forty years.   3 I am *pontifex maximus, augur, quindecimvir sacris faciundis, septemvir epulonum, frater arvalis, sodalis Titius, fetialis.*

8   In my fifth consulship I increased the number of patricians on   BC 29 the instructions of the people and the senate.   2 I revised the roll of the senate three times. In my sixth consulship with Marcus   BC 28

gensimum feci, quo lustro civium Romanorum censa sunt capita quadragiens centum millia et sexaginta tria millia. 3 Tum iterum consulari cum imperio lustrum solus feci C. Censorino et C. Asinio cos., quo lustro censa sunt civium Romanorum capita quadragiens centum millia et ducenta triginta tria millia. 4 Et tertium consulari cum imperio lustrum conlega Tib. Caesare filio meo feci Sex. Pompeio et Sex. Appuleio cos., quo lustro censa sunt civium Romanorum capitum quadragiens centum millia et nongenta triginta et septem millia. 5 Legibus novis me auctore latis multa exempla maiorum exolescentia iam ex nostro saeculo reduxi et ipse multarum rerum exempla imitanda posteris tradidi.

9 Vota pro valetudine mea suscipi per consules et sacerdotes quinto quoque anno senatus decrevit. Ex iis votis saepe fecerunt vivo me ludos aliquotiens sacerdotum quattuor amplissima collegia, aliquotiens consules. 2 Privatim etiam et municipatim universi cives unanimiter continenter apud omnia pulvinaria pro valetudine mea supplicaverunt.

10 Nomen meum senatus consulto inclusum est in saliare carmen, et sacrosanctus in perpetum ut essem et, quoad viverem, tribunicia potestas mihi esset, per legem sanctum est. 2 Pontifex maximus ne fierem in vivi conlegae mei locum, populo id sacerdotium deferente mihi quod pater meus habuerat, recusavi. Quod sacerdotium aliquod post annos, eo mortuo qui civilis motus occasione occupaverat, cuncta ex Italia ad comitia mea confluente multitudine, quanta Romae nunquam fertur ante id tempus fuisse, recepi, P. Sulpicio C. Valgio consulibus.

11 Aram Fortunae Reducis ante aedes Honoris et Virtutis ad portam Capenam pro reditu meo senatus consacravit, in qua pontifices et virgines Vestales anniversarium sacrificium facere iussit eo die quo, consulibus Q. Lucretio et M. Vinicio, in urbem ex Syria redieram, et diem Augustalia ex cognomine nostro appellavit.

Agrippa as colleague, I carried out a census of the people, and I performed a *lustrum* after a lapse of forty-two years; at that *lustrum* 4,063,000 Roman citizens were registered. 3 Then a second time I performed a *lustrum* with consular *imperium* and without a colleague, in the consulship of Gaius Censorinus and Gaius Asinius; BC 8 at that *lustrum* 4,233,000 citizens were registered. 4 Thirdly I performed a *lustrum* with consular *imperium*, with Tiberius Caesar, my son, as colleague, in the consulship of Sextus Pompeius and AD 14 Sextus Appuleius; at that *lustrum* 4,937,000 citizens were registered. 5 By new laws passed on my proposal I brought back into use many exemplary practices of our ancestors which were disappearing in our time, and in many ways I myself transmitted exemplary practices to posterity for their imitation.

9 The senate decreed that vows should be undertaken every fifth year by the consuls and priests for my health. In fulfilment of these vows games have frequently been celebrated in my lifetime, sometimes by the four most distinguished colleges of priests, sometimes by the consuls. 2 Moreover, all the citizens, individually and on behalf of their towns, have unanimously and continuously offered prayers at all the *pulvinaria* for my health.

10 My name was inserted in the hymn of the Salii by a decree of the senate, and it was enacted by law that my person should be inviolable for ever and that I should hold the tribunician power for the duration of my life. 2 I declined to be made *pontifex maximus* in the place of my colleague who was still alive, when the people offered me this priesthood which my father had held. Some years later, after the death of the man who had taken the opportunity of civil disturbance to seize it for himself, I received this priesthood, in the consulship of Publius Sulpicius and Gaius Valgius, and such a BC 12 concourse poured in from the whole of Italy to my election as has never been recorded at Rome before that time.

11 The senate consecrated the altar of Fortuna Redux before the temples of Honour and Virtue at the Porta Capena in honour of my return, and it ordered ·that the *pontifices* and Vestal virgins should make an annual sacrifice there on the anniversary of my return to 12 Oct., the city from Syria in the consulship of Quintus Lucretius and BC 19 Marcus Vinicius, and it named the day the Augustalia from my *cognomen*.

12   Ex senatus auctoritate pars praetorum et tribunorum plebi
cum consule Q. Lucretio et principibus viris obviam mihi missa est
in Campaniam, qui honos ad hoc tempus nemini praeter me est
decretus.   2 Cum ex Hispania Galliaque, rebus in iis provincis
prospere gestis, Romam redi, Ti. Nerone P. Quintilio consulibus,
aram Pacis Augustae senatus pro reditu meo consacrandam censuit
ad campum Martium, in qua magistratus et sacerdotes virginesque
Vestales anniversarium sacrificium facere iussit.

13   Ianum Quirinum, quem claussum esse maiores nostri voluerunt
cum per totum imperium populi Romani terra marique esset parta
victoriis pax, cum, priusquam nascerer, a condita urbe bis omnino
clausum fuisse prodatur memoriae, ter me principe senatus clauden-
dum esse censuit.

14   Filios meos, quos iuvenes mihi eripuit fortuna, Gaium et
Lucium Caesares honoris mei caussa senatus populusque Romanus
annum quintum et decimum agentis consules designavit, ut eum
magistratum inirent post quinquennium, et ex eo die quo deducti sunt
in forum ut interessent consiliis publicis decrevit senatus.   2 Equites
autem Romani universi principem iuventutis utrumque eorum
parmis et hastis argenteis donatum appellaverunt.

15   Plebei Romanae viritim HS trecenos numeravi ex testamento
patris mei et nomine meo HS quadringenos ex bellorum manibiis
consul quintum dedi, iterum autem in consulatu decimo ex patrimonio meo HS quadringenos congiari viritim pernumeravi, et
consul undecimum duodecim frumentationes frumento privatim
coempto emensus sum, et tribunicia potestate duodecimum quadringenos nummos tertium viritim dedi. Quae mea congiaria per-
venerunt ad hominum millia numquam minus quinquaginta et
ducenta.   2 Tribuniciae potestatis duodevicensimum, consul XII,
trecentis et viginti millibus plebis urbanae sexagenos denarios
viritim dedi.   3 Et colonis militum meorum consul quintum ex
manibiis viritim millia nummum singula dedi; acceperunt id
triumphale congiarium in colonis hominum circiter centum et
viginti millia.   4 Consul tertium decimum sexagenos denarios

12   In accordance with the will of the senate some of the praetors and tribunes of the plebs with the consul Quintus Lucretius and the leading men were sent to Campania to meet me, an honour that up to the present day has been decreed to no one besides myself.   **2** On my return from Spain and Gaul in the consulship of Tiberius Nero ʙᴄ 13 and Publius Quintilius after successfully arranging affairs in those provinces, the senate resolved that an altar of the Augustan Peace should be consecrated next to the Campus Martius in honour of my return, and ordered that the magistrates and priests and Vestal virgins should perform an annual sacrifice there.

13   It was the will of our ancestors that the gateway of Janus Quirinus should be shut when victories had secured peace by land and sea throughout the whole empire of the Roman people; from the foundation of the city down to my birth, tradition records that it was shut only twice, but while I was the leading citizen the senate resolved that it should be shut on three occasions.

14   My sons, Gaius and Lucius Caesar, of whom Fortune bereaved me in their youth, were for my honour designated as consuls by the senate and people of Rome when they were fourteen, with the provision that they should enter on that magistracy after the lapse of five years. And the senate decreed that from the day when they were led into the forum they should take part in the councils of state.   **2** Furthermore each of them was presented with silver shields and spears by the whole body of *equites Romani* and hailed as *princeps iuventutis*.

15   To each member of the Roman plebs I paid under my father's ʙᴄ 44 will 300 sesterces, and in my own name I gave them 400 each from the booty of war in my fifth consulship, and once again in my ʙᴄ 29 tenth consulship I paid out 400 sesterces as a largesse to each man ʙᴄ 24 from my own patrimony, and in my eleventh consulship I bought ʙᴄ 23 grain with my own money and distributed twelve rations apiece, and in the twelfth year of my tribunician power I gave every man ʙᴄ 11 400 sesterces for the third time. These largesses of mine never reached fewer than 250,000 persons.   **2** In the eighteenth year of ʙᴄ 5 my tribunician power and my twelfth consulship I gave 240 sesterces apiece to 320,000 members of the urban plebs.   **3** In my fifth consulship I gave 1,000 sesterces out of booty to every one of ʙᴄ 29 the colonists drawn from my soldiers; about 120,000 men in the

plebei quae tum frumentum publicum accipiebat dedi; ea millia
hominum paullo plura quam ducenta fuerunt.

16 Pecuniam pro agris quos in consulatu meo quarto et postea
consulibus M. Crasso et Cn. Lentulo Augure adsignavi militibus
solvi municipis; ea summa sestertium circiter sexsiens milliens fuit
quam pro Italicis praedis numeravi, et circiter bis milliens et sescen-
tiens quod pro agris provincialibus solvi. Id primus et solus omnium
qui deduxerunt colonias militum in Italia aut in provincis ad
memoriam aetatis meae feci. 2 Et postea, Ti. Nerone et Cn. Pisone
consulibus itemque C. Antistio et D. Laelio cos. et C. Calvisio
et L. Pasieno consulibus et L. Lentulo et M. Messalla consulibus et
L. Caninio et Q. Fabricio cos., militibus quos emeriteis stipendis in
sua municipia deduxi praemia numerato persolvi, quam in rem
sestertium quater milliens circiter impendi.

17 Quater pecunia mea iuvi aerarium, ita ut sestertium milliens
et quingentiens ad eos qui praerant aerario detulerim. 2 Et M.
Lepido et L. Arruntio cos. in aerarium militare, quod ex consilio
meo constitutum est ex quo praemia darentur militibus qui vicena
aut plura stipendia emeruissent, HS milliens et septingentiens ex
patrimonio meo detuli.

18 Ab eo anno quo Cn. et P. Lentuli consules fuerunt, cum
deficerent vectigalia, tum centum millibus hominum tum pluribus
multo frumentarios et nummarios tributus ex horreo et patrimonio
meo edidi.

19 Curiam et continens ei Chalcidicum templumque Apollinis in
Palatio cum porticibus, aedem divi Iuli, Lupercal, porticum ad circum Flaminium, quam sum appellari passus ex nomine eius qui
priorem eodem in solo fecerat, Octaviam, pulvinar ad circum
maximum, (2) aedes in Capitolio Iovis Feretri et Iovis Tonantis,
aedem Quirini, aedes Minervae et Iunonis Reginae et Iovis Libertatis in Aventino, aedem Larum in summa sacra via, aedem deum

colonies received this largesse at the time of my triumph. **4** In my thirteenth consulship I gave 60 *denarii* apiece to the plebs who were then in receipt of public grain; they comprised a few more than 200,000 persons.

BC 2

16 I paid cash to the towns for the lands that I assigned to soldiers in my fourth consulship, and later in the consulship of Marcus Crassus and Gnaeus Lentulus. The sum amounted to about 600,000,000 sesterces paid for lands in Italy, and about 260,000,000 disbursed for provincial lands. Of all those who founded military colonies in Italy or the provinces I was the first and only one to have done this in the recollection of my contemporaries. **2** Later, in the consulships of Tiberius Nero and Gnaeus Piso, of Gaius Antistius and Decimus Laelius, of Gaius Calvisius and Lucius Pasienus, of Lucius Lentulus and Marcus Messalla and of Lucius Caninius and Quintus Fabricius I paid monetary rewards to soldiers whom I settled in their home towns after completion of their service, and on this account I expended about 400,000,000 sesterces.

BC 50, 1

BC 7, 6

BC 4

BC 3, 2

17 Four times I assisted the treasury with my own money, so that I transferred to the administrators of the treasury 150,000,000 sesterces. **2** In the consulship of Marcus Lepidus and Lucius Arruntius, when the military treasury was founded by my advice for the purpose of paying rewards to soldiers who had served for twenty years or more, I transferred to it from my own patrimony 170,000,000 sesterces.

6 AD

18 From the consulship of Gnaeus and Publius Lentulus onwards, whenever the taxes did not suffice, I made distributions of grain and money from my own granary and patrimony, sometimes to 100,000 persons, sometimes to many more.

BC 18

19 I built the Senate House, and the Chalcidicum adjacent to it, the temple of Apollo on the Palatine with its porticoes, the temple of the divine Julius, the Lupercal, the portico at the Flaminian circus, which I permitted to bear the name of the portico of Octavius after the man who erected the previous portico on the same site, a *pulvinar* at the Circus Maximus, (2) the temples on the Capitol of Jupiter Feretrius and Jupiter the Thunderer, the temple of Quirinus, the temples of Minerva and Queen Juno and Jupiter Libertas on the Aventine, the temple of the Lares at the top of the

Penatium in Velia, aedem Iuventatis, aedem Matris Magnae in
Palatio feci.

20 Capitolium et Pompeium theatrum utrumque opus impensa
grandi refeci sine ulla inscriptione nominis mei.   **2** Rivos aquarum
compluribus locis vetustate labentes refeci, et aquam quae Marcia
appellatur duplicavi fonte novo in rivum eius inmisso.   **3** Forum
Iulium et basilicam quae fuit inter aedem Castoris et aedem
Saturni, coepta profligataque opera a patre meo, perfeci et eandem
basilicam consumptam incendio, ampliato eius solo, sub titulo nominis filiorum meorum incohavi, et, si vivus non perfecissem, perfici
ab heredibus meis iussi.   **4** Duo et octoginta templa deum in urbe
consul sextum ex auctoritate senatus refeci nullo praetermisso quod
eo tempore refici debebat.   **5** Consul septimum viam Flaminiam ab
urbe Ariminum refeci pontesque omnes praeter Mulvium et
Minucium.

21 In privato solo Martis Ultoris templum forumque Augustum
ex manibiis feci. Theatrum ad aedem Apollinis in solo magna ex
parte a privatis empto feci, quod sub nomine M. Marcelli generi mei
esset.   **2** Dona ex manibiis in Capitolio et in aede divi Iuli et in
aede Apollinis et in aede Vestae et in templo Martis Ultoris consac-
ravi, quae mihi constiterunt HS circiter milliens.   **3** Auri coronari
pondo triginta et quinque millia municipiis et colonis Italiae con-
ferentibus ad triumphos meos quintum consul remisi, et postea,
quotienscumque imperator appellatus sum, aurum coronarium non
accepi decernentibus municipiis et colonis aeque benigne adque
antea decreverant.

22 Ter munus gladiatorium dedi meo nomine et quinquiens
filiorum meorum aut nepotum nomine, quibus muneribus depugna-
verunt hominum circiter decem millia. Bis athletarum undique
accitorum spectaculum populo praebui meo nomine et tertium
nepotis mei nomine.   **2** Ludos feci meo nomine quater, aliorum
autem magistratuum vicem ter et viciens. Pro conlegio XV virorum
magister conlegii collega M. Agrippa ludos saeclares C. Furnio C.

Sacred Way, the temple of the Di Penates in the Velia, the temple of Youth, and the temple of the Great Mother on the Palatine.

20 I restored the Capitol and the theatre of Pompey, both works at great expense without inscribing my own name on either. 2 I restored the channels of the aqueducts, which in several places were falling into disrepair through age, and I brought water from a new spring into the aqueduct called Marcia, doubling the supply. 3 I completed the Forum Julium and the basilica between the temples of Castor and Saturn, works begun and almost finished by my father, and when that same basilica was destroyed by fire, I AD 12 began to rebuild it on an enlarged site, to be dedicated in the name of my sons, and in case I do not complete it in my life time, I have given orders that it should be completed by my heirs. 4 In my sixth consulship I restored eighty-two temples of the gods in the city BC 28 on the authority of the senate, neglecting none that required restoration at that time. 5 In my seventh consulship I restored the BC 27 Via Flaminia from the city as far as Rimini, together with all bridges except the Mulvian and the Minucian.

21 I built the temple of Mars the Avenger and the Forum Augustum on private ground from the proceeds of booty. I built the theatre adjacent to the temple of Apollo on ground in large part bought from private owners, and provided that it should be called after Marcus Marcellus, my son-in-law. 2 From the proceeds of booty I dedicated gifts in the Capitol and in the temples of the divine Julius, of Apollo, of Vesta and of Mars the Avenger; this cost me about 100,000,000 sesterces. 3 In my fifth consulship I remitted 35,000 BC 28 lb. of *aurum coronarium* contributed by the *municipia* and colonies of Italy to my triumphs, and later, whenever I was acclaimed imperator, I refused the *aurum coronarium* which the *municipia* and colonies continued to vote with the same good will as before.

22 I gave three gladiatorial games in my own name and five in that of my sons or grandsons; at these games some 10,000 men took part in combat. Twice in my own name and a third time in that of my grandson I presented to the people displays by athletes summoned from all parts. 2 I produced shows in my own name four times and in place of other magistrates twenty-three times. On behalf of the college of *quindecimviri*, as its president, with Marcus

Silano cos. feci. Consul XIII ludos Martiales primus feci, quos post id tempus deinceps insequentibus annis s.c. et lege fecerunt consules. 3 Venationes bestiarum Africanarum meo nomine aut filiorum meorum et nepotum in circo aut in foro aut in amphitheatris populo dedi sexiens et viciens, quibus confecta sunt bestiarum circiter tria millia et quingentae.

23 Navalis proeli spectaclum populo dedi trans Tiberim in quo loco nunc nemus est Caesarum, cavato solo in longitudinem mille et octingentos pedes, in latitudinem mille et ducenti, in quo triginta rostratae naves triremes aut biremes, plures autem minores inter se conflixerunt; quibus in classibus pugnaverunt praeter remiges millia hominum tria circiter.

24 In templis omnium civitatium provinciae Asiae victor ornamenta reposui quae spoliatis templis is cum quo bellum gesseram privatim possederat. 2 Statuae meae pedestres et equestres et in quadrigeis argenteae steterunt in urbe XXC circiter, quas ipse sustuli, exque ea pecunia dona aurea in aede Apollinis meo nomine et illorum qui mihi statuarum honorem habuerunt posui.

25 Mare pacavi a praedonibus. Eo bello servorum qui fugerant a dominis suis et arma contra rem publicam ceperant triginta fere millia capta dominis ad supplicium sumendum tradidi. 2 Iuravit in mea verba tota Italia sponte sua, et me belli quo vici ad Actium ducem depoposcit; iuraverunt in eadem verba provinciae Galliae, Hispaniae, Africa, Sicilia, Sardinia. 3 Qui sub signis meis tum militaverint fuerunt senatores plures quam DCC, in iis qui vel antea vel postea consules facti sunt ad eum diem quo scripta sunt haec LXXXIII, sacerdotes circiter CLXX.

26 Omnium provinciarum populi Romani quibus finitimae fuerunt gentes quae non parerent imperio nostro fines auxi. 2 Gallias et Hispanias provincias, item Germaniam, qua includit Oceanus a Gadibus ad ostium Albis fluminis pacavi. 3 Alpes a regione ea quae proxima est Hadriano mari ad Tuscum pacificavi nulli genti

Agrippa as colleague, I produced the Secular Games in the consul- BC 17
ship of Gaius Furnius and Gaius Silanus. In my thirteenth consul- BC 2
ship I was the first to produce the games of Mars, which thereafter
in each succeeding year have been produced by the consuls in
accordance with a decree of the senate and by statute.   3 I gave
beast-hunts of African beasts in my own name or in that of my sons
and grandsons in the circus or forum or amphitheatre on twenty-six
occasions, on which about 3,500 beasts were destroyed.

23   I produced a naval battle as a show for the people at the place
across the Tiber now occupied by the grove of the Caesars, where a
site 1,800 feet long and 1,200 broad was excavated. There thirty
beaked triremes or biremes and still more smaller vessels were joined
in battle.   About 3,000 men, besides the rowers, fought in these
fleets.

24   After my victory, I replaced in the temples of all the cities of
the province of Asia the ornaments which my late adversary, after
despoiling the temples, had taken into his private possession.
2 Some eighty silver statues of me, on foot, on horse and in chariots,
had been set up in Rome; I myself removed them, and with the
money that they realized I set golden offerings in the temple of
Apollo, in my own name and in the names of those who had
honoured me with the statues.

25   I made the sea peaceful and freed it of pirates. In that war I
captured about 30,000 slaves who had escaped from their masters
and taken up arms against the republic, and I handed them over to
their masters for punishment.   2 The whole of Italy of its own free
will swore allegiance to me and demanded me as the leader in the
war in which I was victorious at Actium. The Gallic and Spanish
provinces, Africa, Sicily and Sardinia swore the same oath of allegiance.   3 More than seven hundred senators served under my
standards at that time, including eighty-three who previously or
subsequently (down to the time of writing) were appointed consuls,
and about one hundred and seventy who were appointed priests.

26   I extended the territory of all those provinces of the Roman
people on whose borders lay peoples not subject to our government.
2 I brought peace to the Gallic and Spanish provinces as well as to
Germany, throughout the area bordering on the Ocean from Cadiz
to the mouth of the Elbe.   3 I secured the pacification of the Alps

bello per iniuriam inlato. **4** Classis mea per Oceanum ab ostio
Rheni ad solis orientis regionem usque ad fines Cimbrorum naviga-
vit, quo neque terra neque mari quisquam Romanus ante id tempus
adit, Cimbrique et Charydes et Semnones et eiusdem tractus alii
Germanorum populi per legatos amicitiam meam et populi Romani
petierunt. **5** Meo iussu et auspicio ducti sunt duo exercitus eodem
fere tempore in Aethiopiam et in Arabiam quae appellatur Eudae-
mon, magnaeque hostium gentis utriusque copiae caesae sunt in acie
et complura oppida capta. In Aethiopiam usque ad oppidum Nabata
perventum est, cui proxima est Meroe; in Arabiam usque in fines
Sabaeorum processit exercitus ad oppidum Mariba.

27 Aegyptum imperio populi Romani adieci. **2** Armeniam
maiorem interfecto rege eius Artaxe cum possem facere provinciam
malui maiorum nostrorum exemplo regnum id Tigrani regis Arta-
vasdis filio, nepoti autem Tigranis regis, per Ti. Neronem tradere,
qui tum mihi privignus erat. Et eandem gentem postea desciscentem
et rebellantem domitam per Gaium filium meum regi Ariobarzani
regis Medorum Artabazi filio regendam tradidi, et post eius mortem
filio eius Artavasdi; quo interfecto Tigranem qui erat ex regio
genere Armeniorum oriundus in id regnum misi. **3** Provincias
omnis quae trans Hadrianum mare vergunt ad orientem Cyrenas-
que, iam ex parte magna regibus ea possidentibus, et antea Siciliam
et Sardiniam occupatas bello servili reciperavi.

28 Colonias in Africa, Sicilia, Macedonia, utraque Hispania,
Achaia, Asia, Syria, Gallia Narbonensi, Pisidia militum deduxi.
2 Italia autem XXVIII colonias quae vivo me celeberrimae et
frequentissimae fuerunt mea auctoritate deductas habet.

29 Signa militaria complura per alios duces amissa devictis hosti-
bus recepi ex Hispania et Gallia et a Dalmateis. **2** Parthos trium
exercitum Romanorum spolia et signa reddere mihi supplicesque
amicitiam populi Romani petere coegi. Ea autem signa in penetrali
quod est in templo Martis Ultoris reposui.

30 Pannoniorum gentes, quas ante me principem populi Romani
exercitus nunquam adit, devictas per Ti. Neronem, qui tum erat

from the district nearest the Adriatic to the Tuscan sea, yet without waging an unjust war on any people.   4 My fleet sailed through the Ocean eastwards from the mouth of the Rhine to the territory of the Cimbri, a country which no Roman had visited before either by land or sea, and the Cimbri, Charydes, Semnones and other German peoples of that region sent ambassadors and sought my friendship and that of the Roman people.   5 At my command and under my auspices two armies were led almost at the same time into Ethiopia and Arabia Felix; vast enemy forces of both peoples were cut down in battle and many towns captured. Ethiopia was penetrated as far as the town of Nabata, which adjoins Meroë; in Arabia the army advanced into the territory of the Sabaeans to the town of Mariba.

27 I added Egypt to the empire of the Roman people.   2 Greater Armenia I might have made a province after its king, Artaxes had been killed, but I preferred, following the model set by our ancestors, to hand over that kingdom to Tigranes, son of King Artavasdes and grandson of King Tigranes; Tiberius Nero, who was then my stepson, carried this out.   When the same people later rebelled and went to war, I subdued them through the agency of my son Gaius and handed them over to be ruled by King Ariobarzanes, son of Artabazus King of the Medes, and after his death to his son Artavasdes. When he was killed, I sent Tigranes, a scion of the royal Armenian house, to that kingdom.   3 I recovered all the provinces beyond the Adriatic sea towards the east, together with Cyrene, the greater part of them being then occupied by kings. I had previously recovered Sicily and Sardinia which had been seized in the slave war.

28 I founded colonies of soldiers in Africa, Sicily, Macedonia, both Spanish provinces, Achaea, Asia, Syria, Gallia Narbonensis and Pisidia.   2 Italy too has twenty-eight colonies founded by my authority, which were densely populated in my lifetime.

29 By victories over enemies I recovered in Spain and in Gaul, and from the Dalmatians several standards lost by other commanders.   2 I compelled the Parthians to restore to me the spoils and standards of three Roman armies and to ask as suppliants for the friendship of the Roman people. Those standards I deposited in the innermost shrine of the temple of Mars the Avenger.

30 The Pannonian peoples, whom the army of the Roman people never approached before I was the leading citizen, were conquered

privignus et legatus meus, imperio populi Romani subieci, protuli-
que fines Illyrici ad ripam fluminis Danui.   2 Citra quod Dacorum
transgressus exercitus meis auspicis victus profligatusque est, et
postea trans Danuvium ductus exercitus meus Dacorum gentes
imperia populi Romani perferre coegit.

31   Ad me ex India regum legationes saepe missae sunt non visae
ante id tempus apud quemquam Romanorum ducem.   2 Nostram
amicitiam appetiverunt per legatos Bastarnae Scythaeque et Sarma-
tarum qui sunt citra flumen Tanaim et ultra reges, Albanorumque
rex et Hiberorum et Medorum.

32   Ad me supplices confugerunt reges Parthorum Tiridates et
postea Phrates regis Phratis filius, Medorum Artavasdes, Adiabe-
norum Artaxares, Britannorum Dumnobellaunus et Tincommius,
Sugambrorum Maelo, Marcomanorum Sueborum . . . rus.   2 Ad
me rex Parthorum Phrates Orodis filius filios suos nepotesque omnes
misit in Italiam non bello superatus, sed amicitiam nostram per
liberorum suorum pignora petens.   3 Plurimaeque aliae gentes
expertae sunt p. R. fidem me principe quibus antea cum populo
Romano nullum extiterat legationum et amicitiae commercium.

33   A me gentes Parthorum et Medorum per legatos principes
earum gentium reges petitos acceperunt: Parthi Vononem, regis
Phratis filium, regis Orodis nepotem, Medi Ariobarzanem, regis
Artavazdis filium, regis Ariobarzanis nepotem.

34   In consulatu sexto et septimo, postquam bella civilia exstinxe-
ram, per consensum universorum potitus rerum omnium, rem
publicam ex mea potestate in senatus populique Romani arbitrium
transtuli.   2 Quo pro merito meo senatus consulto Augustus
appellatus sum et laureis postes aedium mearum vestiti publice
coronaque civica super ianuam meam fixa est et clupeus aureus in
curia Iulia positus, quem mihi senatum populumque Romanum
dare virtutis clementiaeque et iustitiae et pietatis caussa testatum
est per eius clupei inscriptionem.   3 Post id tempus auctoritate

through the agency of Tiberius Nero, who was then my stepson and legate; I brought them into the empire of the Roman people, and extended the frontier of Illyricum to the banks of the Danube. 2 When an army of Dacians crossed the Danube, it was defeated and routed under my auspices, and later my army crossed the Danube and compelled the Dacian peoples to submit to the commands of the Roman people.

31 Embassies from kings in India were frequently sent to me; never before had they been seen with any Roman commander. 2 The Bastarnae, Scythians and the kings of the Sarmatians on either side of the river Don, and the kings of the Albanians and the Iberians and the Medes sent embassies to seek our friendship.

32 The following kings sought refuge with me as suppliants: Tiridates, King of Parthia, and later Phraates son of King Phraates; Artavasdes, King of the Medes; Artaxares, King of the Adiabeni; Dumnobellaunus and Tincommius, Kings of the Britons; Maelo, King of the Sugambri; . . . rus, King of the Marcomanni and Suebi. 2 Phraates, son of Orodes, King of Parthia, sent all his sons and grandsons to me in Italy, not that he had been overcome in war, but because he sought our friendship by pledging his children. 3 While I was the leading citizen very many other peoples have experienced the good faith of the Roman people which had never previously exchanged embassies or had friendly relations with the Roman people.

33 The Parthian and Median peoples sent to me ambassadors of their nobility who sought and received kings from me, for the Parthians Vonones, son of King Phraates, grandson of King Orodes, and for the Medes, Ariobarzanes, son of King Artavasdes, grandson of King Ariobarzanes.

34 In my sixth and seventh consulships, after I had extinguished BC 28- civil wars, and at a time when with universal consent I was in complete control of affairs, I transferred the republic from my power to the dominion of the senate and people of Rome. 2 For this service of mine I was named Augustus by decree of the senate, and the door-posts of my house were publicly wreathed with bay leaves and a civic crown was fixed over my door and a golden shield was set in the Curia Julia, which, as attested by the inscription thereon, was given me by the senate and people of Rome on account

omnibus praestiti, potestatis autem nihilo amplius habui quam ceteri qui mihi quoque in magistratu conlegae fuerunt.

35 Tertium decimum consulatum cum gerebam, senatus et equester ordo populusque Romanus universus appellavit me patrem patriae, idque in vestibulo aedium mearum inscribendum et in curia Iulia et in foro Aug. sub quadrigis quae mihi ex s.c. positae sunt censuit.   2 Cum scripsi haec annum agebam septuagensumum sextum.

Appendix

1 Summa pecuniae quam dedit vel in aerarium vel plebei Romanae vel dimissis militibus: denarium sexiens milliens.

2 Opera fecit nova aedem Martis, Iovis Tonantis et Feretri, Apollinis, divi Iuli, Quirini, Minervae, Iunonis Reginae, Iovis Libertatis, Larum, deum Penatium, Iuventatis, Matris Magnae, Lupercal, pulvinar ad circum, curiam cum Chalcidico, forum Augustum, basilicam Iuliam, theatrum Marcelli, porticum Octaviam, nemus trans Tiberim Caesarum.

3 Refecit Capitolium sacrasque aedes numero octoginta duas, theatrum Pompei, aquarum rivos, viam Flaminiam.

4 Impensa praestita in spectacula scaenica et munera gladiatorum atque athletas et venationes et naumachiam et donata pecunia colonis, municipiis, oppidis terrae motu incendioque consumptis aut viritim amicis senatoribusque quorum census explevit innumerabilis.

of my courage, clemency, justice and piety. 3 After this time I excelled all in influence, although I possessed no more official power than others who were my colleagues in the several magistracies.

35 In my thirteenth consulship the senate, the equestrian order and the whole people of Rome gave me the title of Father of my Country, and resolved that this should be inscribed in the porch of my house and in the Curia Julia and in the Forum Augustum below the chariot which had been set there in my honour by decree of the senate. 2 At the time of writing I am in my seventy-sixth year. ᴮᶜ 2

Appendix

1 The amount of money that he gave to the treasury or to the Roman *plebs* or to discharged soldiers was 2,400,000,000 sesterces.
2 His new buildings were: the temples of Mars, of Jupiter the Thunderer and Feretrius, of Apollo, of the divine Julius, of Quirinus, of Minerva, of Queen Juno, of Jupiter Libertas, of the Lares, of the Di Penates, of Youth, of the Great Mother, the Lupercal, the shrine at the Circus, the Senate House with the Chalcidicum, the Forum Augustum, the Basilica Julia, the theatre of Marcellus, the Octavian portico, the grove of the Caesars beyond the Tiber.
3 He restored the Capitol and sacred buildings to the number of eighty-two, the theatre of Pompey, the aqueducts and the Via Flaminia.
4 The expenditure that he devoted to dramatic shows, to gladiatorial exhibitions and athletes and hunts and the sea battle, and the money granted to colonies, *municipia*, towns destroyed by earthquake and fire or to individual friends and senators whose property qualification he made up, was beyond counting.

NOTES

Preface. The preamble as it stands in our text was clearly devised for a provincial copy of the *RG*, but it is presumably modelled on the title of the original at Rome: see p. 1.

1,1. Augustus alludes to his raising an army in autumn 44, while still a private citizen. By Caesar's will he had become Caesar's adoptive son and heir and had taken his name, and he aspired to the leadership of the Caesarians. This brought him into rivalry with Antony, then consul, and into temporary collaboration with Republican senators, like Cicero, who saw Antony as a would-be tyrant endangering the liberty of the Roman people. Their aims were quite different from Octavian's; they sympathized with Brutus and Cassius, whom Octavian intended to punish; but Octavian's help was a godsend to them, as they had no troops in Italy and Octavian could raise them by the magic of Caesar's name. He not only called some of Caesar's veterans to his standards but seduced two of Antony's legions. This was wholly illegal, but Cicero was prepared to claim that the safety of the state overrode ordinary legal principles (*Phil.* XI, 28), and from the Republican standpoint at the time Octavian freed Rome from the dominance of Antony's faction; see Syme, pp. 154f., for such propagandist claims and chapters VII–IX for the complicated story of these events. Octavian does not name Antony; indeed he nowhere names any individual Romans, except members of his family, or consuls mentioned for the purpose of dating events.

Considering the illegality of his action in 44 and his *volte face* in 43, when he combined with Antony, an event which he does not mention but which must have been well remembered, we may ask why he chose to record at all that he had raised an army in 44. In the *Res Gestae* omissions are common, and he was not obliged to start in this way. Probably he did so because his claim to have championed the liberty of the Republic provided a keynote for the whole work. It reminded men of his later claim to have preserved the Republic from the despotism of Antony and Cleopatra (EJ, 17, an official dedication to him in 29 by senate and people in the forum) and to have been then the champion of liberty (EJ, 18, a coin of 28). It was easier, in the light of later events, to construe his initial opposition to Antony as the defence of the Republic.

1,2. Octavian's position was legalized by a motion of Cicero on 1 Jan. 43, which granted him the power and honours mentioned here. His *imperium* was that of a praetor, and thus subordinate to that of the consuls, Hirtius and Pansa, old friends of Caesar but opposed to Antony. See Syme, chapters X–XII. For the meaning of *imperium* see p. 83.

1,3. This decree of the senate was also passed on 1 Jan. 43. A similar decree had been passed in many emergencies since 121 BC. Its legal effect is debated. In normal times the *imperium* of magistrates in Rome and Italy was limited by the tribunician veto and by the right of citizens to appeal to the people against arbitrary punishments of execution and flogging. Cicero, however, said that for the consuls 'the safety of the people was the highest law': thus *imperium* gave its holders a residuary power to override laws if the state was in danger. It was easier for them to justify such extraordinary action if the senate as the chief council of state had formally indicated that the state was in danger and authorized them to preserve it from harm; in 121 BC the consul had put citizens to death without trial in such circumstances and had been acquitted when charged with violating their right of appeal. It was probably maintained that citizens who resisted the consuls in such an emergency made themselves by that action into enemies and forfeited citizen rights. In January 43 hostilities had begun in Cisalpine Gaul between Antony and Decimus Brutus, one of Caesar's assassins, and the consuls and Octavian were authorized to take the field against Antony. Naturally, Augustus chooses not to explain the situation fully.

1,4. Nothing is said in detail of the Mutina campaign, in which the consuls defeated Antony but were killed themselves, nor of its aftermath, Octavian's march on Rome which forced the senate to agree to his irregular election to the consulship, and his subsequent compact with Antony and Lepidus, under which he resigned the consulship and became triumvir along with them; the bare facts are recorded without explanation. Octavian's coalition with the Republicans, including his father's assassins, had always been unnatural. A *mot* was ascribed to Cicero that 'the boy was to be praised, honoured and cast aside' (*Fam.* XI, 20); and doubtless this represented the intentions of the Republicans. But Octavian was equally ready to cast aside the senate; he had a large army, which suspected that the senate would deny its promised rewards and gladly followed him against the senate; and this army now placed him on a parity with Antony (whose power had grown again from the support of Lepidus and other commanders beyond the Alps). A deal between them had become possible; all were agreed to establish their own power in the state and to eliminate the true Republicans, notably Brutus and Cassius.

The triumvirate was created by the *lex Titia*, moved by a tribune, which vested the holders with autocratic powers until 1 Jan. 38. Caesar had been autocrat with the title of dictator; after his death the dictatorship was formally abolished for ever; the new law, however, virtually established three dictators. See Syme, chapters XIII–XIV.

From 43 onwards Octavian held *imperium*, first as a propraetor, then as consul, then as triumvir and then again as consul (31–23) and proconsul (after 23). *Imperium* was the legal power in virtue of which he commanded armies and transacted most of his official business. It is sometimes said that he conceals the true nature of his legal power in the *Res Gestae*. If he had done so, it would have been pointless; every one knew the facts. But there is no concealment; he shows clearly enough that he got *imperium* in 43, and his continuous tenure of the power is implied throughout the *Res Gestae*. It is true, of course, that he nowhere sets out explicitly the nature of the Principate; that was not the purpose of this document; it is not a treatise on constitutional law.

2,1. Caesar's killers were condemned by a special tribunal set up by the *lex Pedia* late in 43, after the triumvirs had made themselves masters of Rome. From Augustus' standpoint Brutus and Cassius were murderers and, henceforth, exiles who were making war on the Republic. In their own eyes by killing Caesar they had liberated Rome from a tyrant—tyrannicide was not a crime, but the duty of a citizen—and in 42 they were seeking to free Rome once more from the domination of the triumviral faction.

The two victories are the two battles of Philippi. The first battle was in fact indecisive; while on one wing Antony defeated Cassius' forces, on the other Brutus routed Octavian's and captured his camp. Cassius, ignorant of this success, despaired and killed himself, leaving the command to Brutus, who was a less competent commander; and this action therefore prepared the way for the triumvirs' complete victory in the second action. Naturally Augustus obscures the fact that the first battle had been for him inglorious; the real victor was Antony. For a full narrative of the campaign see Rice Holmes, I, 72–89.

3,1. Augustus calls attention early in his memorial to his victories in war (26–33 n.), and to his clemency. One of his cardinal virtues (34,2), this linked him with Caesar, who had pardoned almost all his opponents. But men spared by Caesar had plotted against him, like Cassius, or condoned his assassination, like Cicero; in 43/2 the triumvirs followed the contrary course, putting to death potential and actual enemies (see Syme, chapter XIV), and acting in the spirit of Cicero's own advice to Brutus: 'if we wish to be merciful, civil wars will never cease' (*ad Brut.* 8, 2). Tacitus thought it important for Augustus' ultimate success that the nobles 'of highest spirit' perished in battle or in the proscriptions (*Ann.* I, 2). Suetonius, *Aug.* 13, says that Octavian showed inflexible rigour in executing captives after Philippi, and Dio LI, 2, that some were put to death after Actium; Augustus himself only claims to have spared those who would beg for mercy (cf. Velleius II, 86). Naturally he says nothing of the proscriptions, and characteristically he uses words which suggest more than they actually state about his clemency. It may be doubted if contemporaries were much impressed with his claim to clemency, as they knew the facts. It was no more than a political catchword (cf. Syme, 159f.). Later, Seneca called the clemency of Augustus 'exhausted cruelty'; cf. Tacitus, *Ann.* I, 10.

3,2. Augustus also claims that he was as merciful as possible to foreign enemies. His words are reminiscent of Virgil's *parcere subiectis et debellare superbos* (*Aen.* VI, 853); Rome's mission was 'to spare the conquered and vanquish the proud in war'. This line might well be read as dividing mankind into those who submitted to Rome and those who refused to submit; the latter Rome was entitled *debellare*. On any view, Augustus' criterion for sparing foreign peoples was the safety of Rome. It was good sense to spare those who would give no more trouble, and pay tribute to Rome.

3,3. Augustus must have counted in the total of 500,000 not only the soldiers he himself raised in 44–31 BC but also those who had been commanded by Lepidus and Antony and surrendered to him in 36 and 31–0, as they were incorporated in his army and took the military oath of obedience to him. Thereafter he had a monopoly of enlisting soldiers, who all took the oath to him. On the other hand, the total of 300,000 to whom he gave lands or money on discharge should not include Antony's veterans discharged after Philippi, for whose settlement in Italy he was only administratively responsible in 41–0.

In AD 14 the citizen units in the Roman army were twenty-five legions, nominally each 6,200 strong (Festus 453 L.), nine praetorian cohorts, each of 1,000 men, and four urban cohorts, said to be 1,500 strong (Tac., *Ann.* IV, 5; cf. III, 41; Dio LV, 24, 6). On the probable assumption that the legions were generally under strength, each about 5,000 men, the total of men serving in these units would have been about 140,000 men. In addition there were some citizens serving in auxiliary units and 7,000 *vigiles*, the fire-brigade at Rome, mainly recruited from freedmen, who counted as soldiers. Before AD 9 there were three more legions, lost under Varus in Germany and not replaced, another 15,000 men.

If the number of soldiers *not* rewarded on discharge by Augustus, *viz.* 200,000, included soldiers serving when he wrote (whether before or after AD 9), it would follow from these estimates that no more than 50,000 had died on service. To judge from mortality in, for instance, the nineteenth century British army in time of peace, this is incredibly low. Evidently, then, Augustus excluded from the total of 500,000 all soldiers still in service when he wrote. On this view two fifths of the total named did not live to the date when discharge was due. The wastage rate is plausible.

In chapter 16 he gives further details of the settlement of veterans. He says that he bought lands for them in 30 and 14 BC and gave them gratuities in cash in 7–2 BC. But he had also settled his own veterans, as well as Antony's, in 41–0, and some others in 36. Of this he says nothing, no doubt because these settlements involved widespread confiscations of land. Moreover, in years he does not mention, and even in those which he cites, some veterans would have been settled in lands sequestered from conquered peoples. Thus, in 25 BC praetorians received allotments at Aosta on lands confiscated from the Salassi (Dio LIII, 25, 5). These grants of land are also ignored in *RG* 16, as they did not constitute a charge on Augustus' purse; and he is there only concerned with his munificence.

In 29 BC veteran colonists already numbered 120,000 (15,3). If these included the survivors of his own soldiers whom Octavian had settled in 41–0 and 36 as well as in 30, the total of soldiers whom he rewarded on discharge after 29 is 180,000. But we cannot be quite sure that the veterans discharged before 30 were included, nor how many they were; a possible, but low, estimate is 40,000, and if they were excluded in 15,3 the total number discharged before 29 was 160,000 and, after 29, 140,000.

In the Republic soldiers served for no fixed term of years and had no recognized claim to land allotments or gratuities in cash on discharge. Only the more fortunate obtained such rewards through the influence of powerful generals under whom they had served. This was the chief reason why armies had been ready to follow their generals against the legal government. Under Augustus, too, veterans at first depended for rewards on his bounty.

At last in 13 BC the period of service was fixed at twelve years for praetorians and sixteen for legionaries, and they were promised definite rewards on discharge (Dio LIV, 25, 5f.). Probably the large number of legionaries demobilized in 14 had served for about sixteen years, replacing some of those disbanded in 30, or recruited even earlier for the Actian war. The men discharged in 7–2 BC might have replaced soldiers raised in the mid 30s and themselves have been discharged after about sixteen years. The new recruits who must have been needed in 14 BC should themselves have been due for discharge in AD 2, or at latest in 6; they could have been retained for four years with lighter duties. But it is doubtful if the government could keep its promises.

Public revenues were evidently insufficient to pay the veterans their due, for in 7–2 BC Augustus had to provide the money from his own resources. In AD 6 a new treasury was established to finance the payment of rewards to veterans (17,2 n.), which were now fixed at 20,000 sesterces for praetorians and 12,000 for legionaries.[1] At the same time the normal period of service was raised to sixteen and twenty years respectively

[1] For the value of the *sestertius*, see p. 57.

(Dio LV, 23, 1; *RG* 17), though legionaries were usually required to
serve an extra five years with lighter duties. Probably the grave revolts,
first in Pannonia (AD 6–8) and then in Germany (AD 9) (*CAH*, X, pp.
369–81, esp. 371 n. 2) as well as lack of funds, made it impossible to
discharge most of the men recruited in 14 BC, while others received not
the gratuities promised but lands which the government bought cheaply
or confiscated in the provinces. In AD 14, just after Augustus' death, there
were serious mutinies on the Rhine and Danube; the mutineers com-
plained that they were kept in service for thirty or forty years and then
fobbed off with grants of marshy or mountainous lands in distant parts
(Tac., *Ann.* I, 17). See Brunt, *Italian Manpower*, 332–42.

3,4.   The ships captured were: more than 300 from Sextus Pompey
in 36 BC (Appian, *B.C.* V, 108; 118) and 300 at Actium (Plutarch,
Antony, 68, quoting Augustus' autobiography). It was normal practice
not to include the numbers of smaller ships captured when recording such
statistics as these.

4,1.   The first ovation, which was shared with Antony, celebrated the
peace of Brundisium in autumn 40 (EJ, p. 33). There was no precedent
for an ovation in such circumstances; it may be explained by the high
hopes which the peace inspired, and which are best illustrated by Virgil's
fourth Eclogue; see Syme, pp. 217ff. The second ovation was for the
victory in a civil war, or one against slaves (25,1; 27,3 with notes). The
greater celebrations of triumphs were on 13–15 August, 29 (EJ, p. 50);
Octavian triumphed on three successive days for his victories in Dalmatia (in 34–3), at Actium and in Egypt; he treated the war of 31/0 as
one with a foreign enemy, the Queen of Egypt. Augustus is known to
have declined triumphs in 25 for victories in Spain and north Italy, in
20–19 after his diplomatic victory over the Parthians (see 29,2 n.) and in
8 BC for victories of Tiberius in Germany.

It was the practice for a victorious general to be hailed *imperator* and
then to wreathe his *fasces* with bay leaves; Augustus dedicated them in
the temple of Capitoline Jupiter in accordance with the vows he had made,
e.g. in 13 BC. *Fasces* were bundles of wooden rods, bound with a red strap,
and including an axe. They symbolized the authority at first of the king,
and then of those magistrates who possessed *imperium*; inside Rome the
axe was removed to show that the magistrates did not have power of life
and death over the citizens. The *fasces* were carried by lictors, who
attended the magistrates, and the number of rods in the bundle varied
with the status of the magistrate.

For Augustus' salutations as *imperator* see 4,2 n.

4,2.   From 27 BC Augustus, as consul or proconsul, governed most of
the provinces in which armies were stationed. He did so through legates

with praetorian *imperium*, which was subordinate to his (pp. 83f.). The legates had not the right to take the auspices, i.e. to consult the gods through the interpretation of omens. That right belonged to Augustus, and therefore the credit for victories they won by the favour of the gods, which he had procured, redounded to him; and for such victories he, not they, was entitled to be hailed *imperator* and to celebrate triumphs; similarly, he can count it to his own glory that the senate offered thanksgivings on such occasions. However, Tiberius and Agrippa were given independent *imperium*. Cf. notes on 6,2 and 30.

4,3. The kings and their children include the two small children of Antony and Cleopatra, Alexander and Cleopatra.

4,4. Augustus was consul in 43, 33, 31–23, 5 and 2 BC. On the importance of this office to him before he abdicated in 23 see p. 9. He took it in 5 and 2 only to introduce his grandsons, Gaius and Lucius, to public life (14,1, notes). His tribunician power was reckoned from 23 BC (p. 10). This section was brought up to date on his death.

5,1–2. The offer of the dictatorship and the corn shortage were directly connected; the shortage went back to 23, when Augustus issued corn at his own cost (15,1), and when his young stepson, Tiberius, was nominally in charge as quaestor (Suet., *Tib.* 8); in 22 the people attributed the shortage to the fact that Augustus had laid down the consulship in 23 after holding it continuously since 31, and violent public agitation forced the senate to offer him the dictatorship (Dio LIV, 1). Augustus went to considerable lengths to persuade the people not to force him to accept the dictatorship: Dio (*loc. cit.*) says that he 'tore his clothes', and Suetonius (*Aug.* 52) that he 'fell to his knees, and dropping his toga, begged them with bared breast'. The reasons are quite clear: Caesar's dictatorship had been deeply resented by the upper classes, and Augustus did not need the power, as Dio notes (*loc. cit.*).

On the other hand, something had to be done about the corn supply; plague and resultant famine had caused this particular crisis, but such crises were frequent. Augustus therefore, like Pompey in 57 BC, accepted a *cura annonae*, supervision of the corn supply, which meant that he took complete charge of the procurement of corn for the capital, and its distribution to those entitled to free corn (see 15 n.); this was the only form of 'poor relief' available in Rome. In accordance with a decree of the senate, Augustus established a commission of ex-praetors, selected by lot, to supervise the *distribution* of corn in the capital. No permanent organization seems to have been set up for *procurement* before another serious famine in AD 6; then and in AD 7 consulars were put in charge (Dio LV, 26, 1–3; 31, 4). Some time between AD 8 and 14 an equestrian prefect, appointed by the emperor and responsible to him, was put in charge of this major problem (cf. Tac., *Ann.* I, 7); distribution of the corn dole remained in the hands of the ex-praetors. There is no mention of this in the *RG*, probably because it was not brought fully up to date in Augustus' last years. It is typical of Augustus' approach to running the state that he tried to solve a difficult problem by employing a remedy for which a Republican precedent existed, and only set up a novel organization after a long lapse of time, when it was shown that the earlier solution was not satisfactory.

5,3. The offer of the consulship, described literally as 'annual and perpetual', that is to say to be granted by election each year, but to be held as an automatic privilege, was presumably an alternative offer to the dictatorship mentioned in 5,1. This too shows how unpopular Augustus' surrender of the consulship was with the ordinary people of Rome. There was probably renewed but unsuccessful agitation for him to hold the consulship again in 21 and 19, when only one consul was elected on each occasion. In both years the offer was refused, but Dio (LIV, 10, 5) may mean that Augustus took consular power for life in 19 BC, cf. pp. 13f.

6,1. It has normally been held that Augustus here directly contradicts Suetonius and Dio. Suetonius (*Aug.* 27) says: 'He also accepted control of morals and laws for life, in virtue of which he three times took the census, although not holding the office of censor.' Dio (LIV, 10, 5) says that on Augustus' return from abroad in 19 BC he was made 'supervisor of morals for five years, and took censorial powers for the same period'. Dio adds (LIV, 30, 1) that his powers as supervisor of morals were renewed for a further five years (ἔτερα ἔτη πέντε) in 12 BC. *Suetonius* is inconsistent with Dio in saying that Augustus took these powers for life, and with Augustus himself (8,2–4) in explaining the census procedure; there is no reason why Augustus should have falsified this point, and Suetonius is probably wrong on the duration of the powers as well. However, there is nothing in *Dio* which is necessarily inconsistent with what Augustus says. Augustus claims that he refused 'any office inconsistent with the custom of our ancestors'; that would exclude an office of supervisor of morals *summa potestate*, 'with supreme power', which implies a virtual dictatorship, but there would be nothing essentially unrepublican in Augustus holding a supervision of morals, which was a normal part of the office of the censors, and Augustus does not categorically deny that he took *any* sort of supervision of morals or censorial power. Dio does not state that the second tenure of these powers was consecutive on the first, and there need therefore be no contradiction in his dates, though that of 12 BC should presumably be altered to 11 in accord with Augustus' statement here. It may be significant that the grants recorded by Dio in 19 and

12 are each followed closely by a revision of the list of the senate (8,2–4 n.). See further, Jones, chapter II.

Dio's assertion that Augustus received special grants of censorial power must also be considered in connexion with the Augustan censuses (8,2–4). The Fasti of Venusia (EJ, p. 35) state that he and Agrippa took the census of 28 BC in virtue of censorial power. Augustus merely says that he and Agrippa took it 'in my sixth consulship'. This may be a mode of dating the census; it does not imply that Augustus and Agrippa took it *as consuls*. Legally, consuls were no doubt competent to take a census, as they were believed to have done in the fifth century; but it would certainly have been a breach with long existing practice if they had done so without other authority. This authority might have been given them by a decree of the senate inviting them to use their consular power for performing censorial duties; and this may be the truth underlying the statement in the Fasti. Similar decrees might have authorized Augustus alone in 8 BC, and Augustus and Tiberius in AD 14, to take censuses. Augustus says that these censuses were taken 'with consular *imperium*', and we agree with Jones (p. 15) that this supports his hypothesis that Augustus could exercise consular powers in Rome and Italy at the relevant dates (see p. 13). But if Augustus and Agrippa, even when actually consuls, had felt it necessary to obtain special authority to perform censorial functions, it seems likely that Augustus would also have obtained it on the later occasions, when he was not consul, but only the equal of the consuls. In other words, the *imperium* gave him the legal capacity to take a census, but he would have wished to secure sanction for using that *imperium* in a particular way, which was untraditional. The census of 8 BC falls within Dio's second quinquennium of censorial power. As for AD 14, the law that authorized Tiberius to take the census with Augustus (Suet., *Tib.* 21) may also have given Augustus himself the authority to act.

6,2. The measures which Augustus claims the senate wished him to carry out were aimed at restoring the moral basis of society. The moral decline in the late Republic was commented on by many authors: Livy (Preface, 12) says: 'recently wealth has introduced greed, and abundant pleasures a longing to ruin and destroy everything through luxury and immorality'. Sallust dates the moral crisis in Rome from the destruction of Carthage (146 BC), and gives the fullest analysis of its causes in *Catiline* 10–12; other Roman authors favour a date earlier in the second century. Julius Caesar was expected to do something about the situation (Cic., *pro Marc.* 23), and the expectations appear again when Augustus became established in power; see, for instance, Horace, *Odes* III, 6; 24. In particular it was necessary to encourage marriage among the upper classes to check a falling birth rate. Apparently Augustus made some abortive proposal on this subject before 23. In 18 BC came the *Leges Juliae de maritandis ordinibus* and *de adulteriis*, 'Julian Laws on the Marriage of the Orders and on Adultery'. This legislation was not by any means totally successful, nor was it popular; one may suspect that Augustus was not utterly frank when he said that the senate wished him to pass it. These laws punished adultery and laid down penalties for those who were unmarried, and privileges for those with three children. See *CAH* X, 441ff., and the important article of G. Williams in *J.R.S.* LII (1962), 28ff.

At the same time Augustus passed a new law against electoral bribery. This shows that he did not control all elections; no one would waste money on corrupting voters, if the result was a foregone conclusion.

All these laws Augustus passed through the plebeian assembly in virtue of his tribunician power, for which see p. 11. The marriage law was amended in AD 9 by the *Lex Papia Poppaea*, promoted by the consuls. This shows how later he preferred to get consuls to sponsor his measures.

Augustus adds that he took colleagues in the tribunician power. Collegiality was one of the essential features of the Republican system; see 34,3 n. Augustus is suggesting once more, as in 5,1 and 6,1, that he was far from seeking a monarchical position. The tribunician power was granted to his son-in-law, Agrippa, for five years in 18 and 13 BC; he died in 12. Tiberius received it as Augustus' stepson in 6 BC, but then retired to Rhodes (cf. 14,1 n.); the grant expired in 1 BC and was not renewed. But he received a new grant in AD 4, when he was adopted, and this was renewed in 13. Unlike Augustus, neither Agrippa nor Tiberius received the power for life. But, as the 'title of the highest eminence', it marked out each of them in turn as virtually the heir presumptive to Augustus. Hence, Velleius (II, 99, 1) describes Tiberius as 'made the equal of Augustus by sharing the tribunician power'.

However, the tribunician power was not the real basis of Augustus' control (cf. pp. 12f), and it did not suffice for Agrippa or Tiberius. In 19 and 14 BC Agrippa was voted a triumph, which he did not celebrate (Dio LIV, 11, 6; 24, 7); this implies that he was more than a legate and had independent *imperium*, as does the fact that he bore the title of *imperator* (EJ, 71; 75); cf. 4,1 n. The language of Dio (LIV, 12, 4 and 28, 1) may suggest that on the occasions when he received tribunician power he also secured *imperium maius* throughout the empire. Tiberius had perhaps obtained independent *imperium* even before tribunician power (30 n.); he certainly possessed it in AD 4. Inscriptions show that he shared seven of Augustus' salutations as *imperator*, and he triumphed in AD 12. Until then, his *imperium* was probably restricted to the provinces where he was actually in command, but now, according to Velleius (II, 121, 1), he was given rights equal to those of Augustus in all provinces and armies, and

according to Suetonius (*Tib.* 21), authorized to administer the provinces
and take the census jointly with Augustus (6,1 n.). On Augustus' death
he thus already possessed the reality of power. See Addenda, p. 81

7,1.   Octavian, Antony and Lepidus were first made triumvirs (cf. 1,4
and note) up to 31 Dec. 38; this is known from an inscription (EJ, p. 32).
They continued to hold the power in 37 without formally renewing it
until the autumn; they then agreed to take a second term of five years
and probably secured the subsequent approval of the assembly at Rome.
Did this second 'quinquennium' run retroactively from the beginning of
37 to the last day of 33, or for a period of a little more than five years
from the time of renewal to the last day of 32 ? Appian (*Illyrian Wars* 28)
categorically asserts the second view, but cannot be trusted implicitly on
such points. Augustus' own statement favours the first view. If he had
merely said that he held office for ten years, it would have been easy to
suppose that those years consisted of the quinquennium Nov. 43–Dec. 38
plus the quinquennium late 37–Dec. 32 and that he conveniently passed
over in silence the intervening months, in which he and his colleagues had
retained the power without statutory authority. But he claims to have
held the power for ten *consecutive* years. Even this claim is somewhat
economical of the truth, since it ignores what is a fact on this hypothesis,
that the legal term expired before formal renewal and that the gap was
only made good by retroactive legislation. But this kind of omission is
venial and characteristic of Augustus. On the other hand, if the other
view is right, his statement is not only untruthful but a purposeless lie,
since the facts would have been well known to his readers.

The evidence of the Capitoline *Fasti*, inscribed in Augustus' reign, also
favours the terminus in 33. These give a list of magistrates; unfortunately
names survive for only two years in the triumviral period, 37 and 36.
Now the names of the triumvirs stand at the head of the entry for 37 and
not for 36. The most natural explanation is that they were recorded only
for the year in which the second term was retrospectively deemed to have
begun. In that case the second term ended in Dec. 33.

Various other arguments have been adduced to support each hypothesis, but in our view all are inconclusive. One point is of special importance. In 32 (probably in February) Octavian took his seat in the senate
between the consuls (Dio L, 2, 5). This symbolized a claim to be the equal
or superior of the consuls. But at the time he held no office, unless he was
still triumvir. This does not necessarily imply that, despite the evidence
of this chapter and of the *Fasti Capitolini*, his second term did not run out
till December 32. In 37 all the triumvirs had continued in office after the
expiry of the first term for several months before renewing their power.
Antony purported to be triumvir in 31, when on any view the second
term was over. It can be argued that a magistrate did not lay down office

until he formally abdicated (as the consuls did each year) and that the triumvirs, who could not be compelled to abdicate, could legally retain their office beyond the time appointed by the statute under which they received it.

Did Octavian then retain the triumvirate after the expiry of the second term? It is certain that he ceased to call himself triumvir, but he is not known to have abdicated, and it would have been at least uncertain whether he did not still possess the power. Since Lepidus had been deposed and Antony was in arms against the Republic, the name of triumvir was inapposite, and that may help to explain why Octavian did not parade the title, though still exercising the authority. Until 28/7 he remained by his own admission in absolute control of the state and superior to his colleagues in the consulship in 31–29; and this fact *can* be explained by the supposition that he remained triumvir in fact, though not in name, right down to the great abdication in January 27 (cf. 34,1 and note).

If this view is correct, then Octavian was really triumvir for fifteen years, not ten; and his own statement here, relating simply to the period in which he held the office in accordance with statutes, is highly misleading. But it is the kind of misleading assertion he was capable of making, as it was in one sense true.

7,2. The title *princeps senatus*, 'leading member of the senate', is not to be confused with *princeps* on its own, which was the term by which the emperors came to style their position. *Princeps senatus* was a normal Republican title, given to the member of the senate who was first asked his opinion by the presiding magistrate, and Augustus took it in 28 BC at the time of his first revision of the list of the senate. The Greek translation is here informative, πρῶτον ἀξιώματος τόπον, 'leading position of authority', since ἀξίωμα (authority) is used as the translation of *auctoritas*; see p. 84 f., and 34,2–3 nn. The title *princeps iuventutis*, 'chief of the young men', which was granted to Gaius and Lucius Caesar, was new, and a purely honorific title; see 14,2 note.

7,3. Augustus here records his membership of the great priestly colleges. Membership was not incompatible with high offices of state: on the contrary, it generally fell to the men whose rank and political careers were most distinguished; indeed magistrates themselves sacrificed and obtained signs of the will of the gods. The *pontifices* presided over and advised on the state cults in general; as the head of the college (cf. 10,2) Augustus also had certain disciplinary powers over other priests, notably the Vestal Virgins (11–12,1 n). It was the duty of the *augures* to interpret signs by which the gods were thought to declare whether or not they approved of a proposed official action. The *quindecimviri* supervised those foreign cults which from very early times had been adopted at Rome, especially Greek cults like that of Apollo. The *septemviri epulonum* organized public banquets in honour of the gods. The *fratres Arvales* celebrated an ancient agricultural rite; their hymn, which is preserved, is one of the earliest extant pieces of Latin and must have been unintelligible by this time; we have also numerous fragments of their proceedings in the Principate which show that they were then mainly concerned with prayers and sacrifices for the well-being of the imperial house. The *sodales Titii* are obscure. The *fetiales* were concerned in the making of treaties and in declarations of war; in the first case they invoked a curse on Rome if she were the first to break the treaty; in the second they appealed to the gods to hear that Rome's cause was just. See the articles in *OCD*.

It was a mark of Augustus' special position that he belonged to all these colleges; the most eminent Romans in the Republic seldom held more than one priesthood. In the Republic the first three colleges had been often of political importance, with some power to promote or obstruct proposals in accordance with their own views. Augustus did not need to use these devices to get his own way, but, apart from the honour which came to him from being a member of each of the colleges, it was one of his aims to revive respect for the old religious practices, and by himself holding the priesthoods named, he enhanced their importance. It was characteristic, for instance, that he personally employed the old ritual of the *fetiales* in declaring war on Cleopatra (Dio, L, 4, 4). See Suetonius, *Aug.* 31 and *CAH* X, 475ff.

8,1. The patricians were Rome's earliest aristocracy. Until the fourth century they monopolized offices and priesthoods. When this monopoly ended and plebeians were admitted to offices, a new 'nobility' grew up, which included the descendants of plebeian consuls as well as patricians. In Augustus' day the distinction between patricians and plebeians had no political importance, but some priesthoods were still reserved to patricians, and as they were dying out, he took powers under a *lex Saenia* to enrol more. The measure illustrates his respect for religious traditions.

8,2–4. In the late Republic the senate was normally about 600 strong; by 29 it had swollen to 1,000. In 29 Augustus revised the list; he persuaded fifty senators whom he thought unworthy to retire, and excluded 140 more. In 18 he wished to reduce the number still further and at first tried a complicated procedure under which senators co-opted each other, but in the end he made up the list himself. Suetonius (*Aug.* 35) mentions only these two *lectiones* and reverses the order, correctly given in Dio (LII, 42, 1ff.; LIV, 13f.). Dio also mentions three more, in 13 BC (LIV, 26, 3), 11 BC (LIV, 35, 1) and AD 4 (LV, 13, 3); of these the last is clearly not included by Augustus among those he carried out himself, as the task was entrusted to a commission of senators. Jones (pp. 22f.)

argues that Dio's record for 13 BC is based on a misunderstanding; in that case the third occasion on which Augustus revised the roll of the senate was in 11. All these *lectiones* were extraordinary; normally men entered the senate automatically after holding the quaestorship.

A *lustrum* was a ceremony of purification, normally a procession, which at one time had had a magical meaning. It was carried out by censors when they had taken the census. See further Warde Fowler, *Religious Experience of the Roman People*, pp. 209ff.

The last Republican census recorded was in 70 BC, when 910,000 citizens were registered. This total should have included all male citizens aged over seventeen, but it was probably very incomplete. By 28 BC numbers had apparently quadrupled. This is a puzzle. There was no such rate of growth in the second century BC, nor between 28 BC and AD 14, yet these were more peaceful periods; between 70 and 28 the constant wars and devastations should have been unfavourable to natural increase, and in fact contemporaries expressed alarm at the decline of population. It is true that numbers had certainly grown in ways other than natural increase. All the time numerous slaves were being manumitted by citizens and acquiring citizenship thereby. In 49 the freeborn people of the Po valley were enfranchised. No doubt many provincials secured citizenship. It has also been argued that Augustus' enumeration in 28 was much more efficient than that in 70; this need not be so. But scholars who believe that Augustus only registered adult males, even after making handsome allowances for all these factors, are still obliged to posit an 'explosion' of population, which seems quite implausible. It is better, then, to adopt the view of K. J. Beloch that Augustus included women and some children, and that the figures for his reign are not directly comparable with Republican figures. The total population of Italy can only be guessed from these data. Including slaves, it might have amounted to 7–8 millions. See Brunt, *Italian Manpower*, Part I, especially chapters IX–X.

The *Fasti* of Ostia (EJ, p. 40) give a return of only 4,100,900 for AD 14. This figure must represent an enumeration less complete than that finally returned.

The growth in recorded numbers from 28 BC to AD 14 may indicate improved efficiency in taking the census, and an influx of newly enfranchised citizens, formerly slaves or provincials, rather than natural increase among the old citizens. The marriage laws (6,2 n.) only concerned a fraction of the old citizens, men of property and freedmen, and could have had no effect in raising the general birth-rate.

On the powers in virtue of which Augustus took the censuses see 6,1 n. It may be added that if sections 3 and 4 show that Augustus acted in virtue of a consular *imperium* which was operative in Italy, section 4 should prove, *contra* Jones, p. 16, that in AD 14 Tiberius' *imperium* was also operative there in the lifetime of Augustus. Jones adduces against this view the fact that immediately after Augustus' death Tiberius convened the senate in virtue of tribunician power (Tac., *Ann.* I, 7); but this does not show that he lacked *imperium* in Rome and Italy; there is no ground for thinking that Augustus too did not summon meetings in virtue of tribunician power, extended for him in the way described on p. 11. Tiberius was giving orders to the troops in Rome at the same time.

8,5. Augustus refers chiefly to his moral legislation (cf. 6,2). The respect he expresses for tradition is typical of his professions, perhaps of his real beliefs. A Roman could properly seek to build further on tradition. The elder Cato had ascribed the special excellence of the Republican constitution to its having been evolved by the wisdom of many successive generations (Cic., *de Rep.* II, 2), and Livy argued that innovation in the interest of the state was itself part of the Roman tradition (IV, 4). Thus respect for tradition did not need to inhibit Augustus from setting new precedents.

9,1. The four colleges were those of the pontifices, augurs, quindecimvirs and septemvirs; see 7,3 n.

9,2. At certain ceremonies of Greek origin statues of the gods were brought from their temples to partake of a sacred banquet, and laid on cushioned couches, *pulvinaria*, like those on which Romans lay when they dined.

10,1. The hymn of the Salii, an ancient priesthood, was an incantation accompanied by a dance, designed originally to ensure the safety of Rome in war. The inclusion of Augustus' name in the hymn indicated that the safety of Rome was considered to be bound up with his safety. It also placed him on a par with the gods. L. R. Taylor, *Divinity of the Roman Emperor*, p. 236, remarks that this is the only quasi-divine honour Augustus mentions.

The inviolability of tribunes was believed to go back to an oath taken by plebeians and embodied in a law, which entitled any one to kill with impunity a person who outraged a tribune. On Augustus' tribunician power see pp. 10ff.

10,2. On the death of Caesar, who had been *pontifex maximus*, this priesthood was secured, rather irregularly, by Lepidus, the later triumvir. Augustus refused to deprive him of the priesthood in 36, when he deposed him from the triumvirate; there would have been no precedent for deprivation. Lepidus lived on in retirement until 13 BC, and Augustus, who had belonged to the college of pontifices as early as 36, at last succeeded him in 12. Appointment had been by popular election since the third century. Augustus' words here do not confirm Dio's statement (XLIV, 5, 3) that the chief pontificate had been made hereditary in

Caesar's time; had this been so, as Caesar's adoptive son, he could have treated Lepidus as a usurper. He is concerned to emphasize his strict regard for legality, and the strength of the popular demand throughout Italy that he should assume the priesthood, which made him a kind of head of the state religion.

11–12,1. During Augustus' absence from Rome in 22–19 BC there were serious disorders. In particular, M. Egnatius Rufus, who had gained popularity by forming a private fire-brigade, stood illegally for the consulship of 19, was held guilty of treason and was put to death in prison. Only one consul had been elected (C. Sentius Saturninus, who suppressed Egnatius); Q. Lucretius, named in 12,1, was 'appointed' by Augustus to fill the vacancy, when he had been sent as a member of the senatorial deputation to Augustus in Campania (Dio LIV, 10, 2); doubtless he was formally elected in compliance with Augustus' will; see Syme, pp. 371f. The altar set up by the Porta Capena, the gate by which Augustus entered Rome, to the goddess Fortune who had brought him back safely ('Redux') and the annual celebrations here mentioned symbolized the relief felt by the citizens at his return and at the restoration of order. For new honours or powers granted to Augustus at this time and not mentioned here see pp. 13f.

Vesta was the divine spirit of the hearth, whether that of the family or of the state; in primitive times it was of great importance to keep a fire going, and the cult of the spirit of the hearth arose from this cause. The state cult was committed to six Vestal Virgins under the supervision of the *pontifex maximus*. See the article in *OCD*.

12,2. Augustus was again absent in 16–13 BC; the altar of the Augustan Peace and the annual celebrations commemorated his return. For the sculptural fragments generally thought to belong to this altar see *CAH* X, 546ff.; they are the most important iconographic evidence for Augustan ideals and propaganda. They show Augustus performing priestly duties, accompanied by his family; this illustrates his dynastic hopes, as well as the importance he attached to the old religion. There is a procession of senators and citizens, in relation to whom Augustus appears as first citizen rather than as monarch. Children appear in the processions, and not only among the imperial family; they may symbolize the hopes of a rising birth-rate among the higher classes. A seated figure with children and fruits on her lap and animals at her feet may personify either Italy or the bountiful Earth-Mother; even if the second identification is right, Italians would surely have seen her as a symbol of the bounty of their own country. Another figure, only partly preserved, may have personified Rome. Representations of the arrival of Aeneas in Italy and of the nurture of Romulus connected the new age with the remote past, and festoons of fruit and flowers suggested the plenty it had brought. The sculptures are illustrated in *CAH, Vol. of Plates* IV, pp. 112ff. and more fully by J. M. C. Toynbee, *Ara Pacis Reconsidered, Proc. of Brit. Academy*, 1953, 67ff. (obtainable separately). S. Weinstock *JRS* L (1950) denies that the sculptures belong to the altar of Peace, but see J. M. C. Toynbee, *ibid.* LI (1951), 153ff.). M. Rostovtseff, *Soc. and Econ. Hist. of the Roman Empire* I, 44f. (with plates) compares an altar in a temple of the Augustan family at Carthage, which shows Rome holding a pillar with a *clupeus* (34,2 n.), brought down from heaven by Victory; before the goddess stands an altar with horns of plenty and a globe; the idea is that under Augustus' leadership Rome is to secure world-wide peace and prosperity (see notes on 13 and 26–33).

13. Janus seems to have been originally the divine power (*numen*) which, men thought, resided in and protected a door or the city gates, and Quirinus to have been a local spirit of the Quirinal hill, who later emerged as a god of war; see the articles in *OCD*. The name Janus Quirinus was apparently used of an arched gate near the Palatine. The view that it was only to be closed when universal peace prevailed goes back to the historian, Lucius Calpurnius Piso (consul 133 BC), and the antiquarian Varro, a contemporary of Cicero, had said that it had only twice been closed in Roman history. Rome was certainly at peace on more than two occasions, but the assertion was accepted by Augustus. His own closures memorably symbolized his success in pacifying the Roman world, a success which did more than anything else to consolidate his power; as Tacitus said, 'he seduced every one by the delights of peace' (*cunctos dulcedine otii pellexit*), and 'it was in the interest of peace that all power should be conferred on one man' (*Ann.* I, 2; *Hist.* I, 1). After the turmoil of the civil wars which had engulfed Italy and almost every province in bloodshed and heavy financial exactions, the importance of this achievement to the ordinary individual can hardly be exaggerated; Horace says: *ego nec tumultum/nec mori per vim metuam tenente/Caesare terras*, 'with Caesar guarding the lands I will not fear commotions or death by violence'; *Odes* III, 14, 14ff.) and in AD 14 Alexandrine sailors honoured Augustus 'because it was through him that they lived and sailed the sea and enjoyed their freedom and fortunes' (Suet., *Aug.* 98). More pompous expression was given to the same idea by the provincial council of Asia, which declared in 9 BC that divine providence had granted Caesar to them and their posterity as a Saviour, who had made war to cease and was to establish a peaceful order; his Epiphany had transcended the hopes of all who had anticipated the good tidings; the birth of the new god inaugurated a better age (EJ, 98 (b)). Cf. 22,2 n.

Janus was first closed in January 29 after the end of the civil war, and again in 25, after the suppression of the Cantabrians in Spain. Though the Romans had governed Spain for nearly 200 years, the country was first

thoroughly pacified by Augustus, as Velleius noted (II, 90); we have an
inscription set up to him at Rome by the province of Baetica after 2 BC,
'because the province has been pacified by his aid and unceasing care'
(EJ, 42); however, the work was not quite finished in 25. The third
closure is of unknown date; the Christian historian, Orosius (VI, 22) put
it in 2 BC, but at that time there was a war with Parthia. Orosius was
suggesting that when Christ was born 'no war or battle's sound / was
heard the world around'! (The Roman peace was in fact one of the
conditions that facilitated Christian evangelism.)

Peace was secured by *victories*; its glorification was therefore not incompatible with the emphasis Augustus lays on his military achievements (see 26ff. and notes). *Pax* means 'pacification' as much as 'no
fighting'. But the citizen who enjoyed security at home could also take
pride in the extension of Roman power to distant regions where Rome
imposed peace.

Here, as in 30,1 and 32,3, Augustus refers to himself as *princeps*, the
leading man at Rome, a compendious term to describe a position which
rested on various and complex legal powers and on his *auctoritas* (pp. 84f
and 34,3 n.). Hence ancient and modern writers use the term 'principate'
to describe the veiled monarchy which Augustus founded. In the Republic the most influential senators had been described as *principes*, as
indeed Augustus himself describes such men in 12,1. It was a novelty
that one man could call himself '*princeps*' *par excellence*, yet the word
had sufficient Republican flavour to make its use in this way not too
overtly monarchical.

14,1.   Gaius and Lucius Caesar were the sons of Agrippa by Augustus'
only child, Julia. Born in 20 and 17 BC respectively, they were adopted by
Augustus in 17, and he assumed the consulship to lead Gaius into the
forum in 5 and Lucius in 2 BC (4,4 n.); at the age of fifteen each was
deemed to have reached his majority, and to be competent to take part in
public affairs. Gaius was designated for the consulship of AD 1, which he
held, and Lucius for that of AD 4; but he died in AD 2. Already in 1 BC
Gaius had received nominal command first of the Danubian legions, and
then of those in the east (Dio LV, 10, 17f.); he was of course accompanied
by experienced advisers. In a letter to Gaius, preserved by Aulus Gellius
(XV, 7), Augustus looks forward to the time when his grandsons would
take over his position in the state. The extraordinary honours they received made his hopes patent. Both were to be consuls when only twenty-
one; the earliest age for other Romans in the Principate was thirty-two,
and forty-two was perhaps more common (Syme, *Tacitus* II, pp. 653ff.).
By taking Agrippa as his partner (6,2 n.), Augustus had doubtless hoped
to mark out a regent to hold power for them if he himself died before his
grandsons reached maturity. Unfortunately, Agrippa died in 12. In 6 BC

Augustus turned to his stepson, Tiberius, who had contracted a loveless marriage with Julia, and made him partner in the tribunician power. Presumably Tiberius was cast in the same role as Agrippa, and this was made clear by the fact that the extraordinary honours mentioned here were voted in the same year. This was a part Tiberius would not play: almost at once he retired in dudgeon to Rhodes, where he became a virtual exile, in some danger from Gaius' hostility. He returned to Rome in AD 2, but only with Gaius' consent, and to live in retirement. But in AD 4 Gaius died of wounds. At last Augustus adopted Tiberius as his son, saying that he did so 'for the good of the state' (Vell. II, 104), and made him almost co-ruler (6,2 n.). In his will he explained that he had made Tiberius heir to his property because 'a cruel fate has torn from me my sons Gaius and Lucius' (Suet., *Tib.* 23). If the new régime was to be stable, Augustus had to leave an experienced successor with powers that would ensure a smooth take-over; but it is clear that he felt no affection for Tiberius, and fell back upon him only as a last resort. What he really desired most of all was a dynastic succession. This ambition was natural to a Roman; every noble hoped that his descendants would reach the same dignity as himself. Even in AD 4 Augustus did not give up this aim. Tiberius had a grown son, the younger Drusus, yet was made to adopt his nephew, Germanicus, who was but little older. The reason is not hard to seek: Germanicus had married Agrippina, the daughter of Agrippa and Julia, and their sons were the great-grandsons of Augustus. See Syme, pp. 415–18; 427–31.

14,2. The *equites Romani* were those citizens of free birth and a minimum property qualification of 400,000 sesterces who had been given, as a distinction, the right to a horse at the public cost, and who were enrolled in 18 'centuries' (voting units in the Roman assembly). They included, besides young men of senatorial family who had not yet entered the senate, the richest of the other citizens. The great tax-farmers of the Republic were drawn from their midst, and they provided judges for the courts, and in the Principate an increasing proportion of military officers and administrators. They were entitled to special dress and special seats at public shows. Augustus took great pains with their enrolment; those under thirty-five were expected to parade before him on horse each year (Suet., *Aug.* 38). Though not all of them were young, those who paraded generally were, and it was therefore not inappropriate that they should designate the young Caesars as 'chiefs of the youth'; this title had been unofficially bestowed on C. Scribonius Curio in his twenties by Cicero in 56 (*in Vat.* 24). It is, however, something of a novelty that here and in 35 we find the *equites* acting as an organized 'order'.

The term 'youth' should denote the period when men were liable for active service as *iuniores* (from seventeen to forty-six, or perhaps now thirty-five, when Augustus allowed *equites* to surrender the public horse). The Caesars were below that age, but it was no more anomalous to make them heads of the equestrian order when boys than to make them nominal heads of the state (as consuls) long before the legal age. There is some evidence that Augustus encouraged boys of the upper class to pursue gymnastic, equestrian and military exercises (cf. Horace, *Odes* I, 8; III, 2; 12 and 24), such as the dangerous *lusus Troiae* (Suet., *Aug.* 43), described in *Aeneid* V, 553ff.; and clubs of *iuvenes*, widely found in Italy, were probably intended for such exercises. But it is a superfluous conjecture that the honour bestowed by the *equites* on the Caesars has any connexion with these matters.

15–24. *Excursus on Augustus' expenditure*

In these chapters Augustus records his *impensae*, the moneys he spent from his *private* wealth for the good of the state or its citizens. The sums are given in sesterces. It would be unrealistic to try to give modern monetary equivalents, since we do not know what the *sestertius* could buy. The best way of evaluating Augustus' munificence is to set the figures he gives alongside other Roman figures. The legionary in his day received 900 *sesterces* a year, out of which deductions were made for the cost of his food, arms, and clothing. The minimum property qualification for a senator was one million, but Pompey's landed property was valued at 200 millions; he also lent out immense sums. By his conquests in the east Pompey also added 340 millions to public revenues. Total revenue under Augustus is unknown.

Augustus gives only a selection of his benefactions. He is concerned mainly with his gifts to the urban plebs, to soldiers and to the treasury, with buildings and shows in the city of Rome, and to a lesser extent with benefactions in Italy. He neglects many other liberalities, especially in the provinces; see Appendix and notes.

In 44 Augustus paid out 75 millions or more to the Roman plebs under Caesar's will (15,1). Between that time and Actium there is little to record; the portico of the Flaminian circus was built in 33, but work on the senate-house and the temple of Julius, begun in 42, and on the temple of Apollo on the Palatine, begun in 36, was not finished before 29/8 (19,1), and the temple of Mars Ultor, begun in 42, was not dedicated until 2 BC (21,1).

But in 30–27 there was prodigious expenditure, probably the larger part of the 860 millions spent in buying lands for veterans (16,1), 220 millions on gifts to the urban plebs and to veterans (15,1 and 3), 100 millions on dedications in temples (21,2); in 28 BC, Augustus renounced the equivalent of 147 millions by remitting the free will offerings of Italian towns (21,3). Two of his eight gladiatorial shows belong to 29 and 28 (22,1 n.). Apart from the completion of the buildings mentioned above, he constructed at this time the shrine at the Circus Maximus and the Capitoline temple of Jupiter Feretrius (19), repaired all the eighty-two dilapidated temples (20,4) and rebuilt the Via Flaminia, the highway to the north, with all its bridges (20,5). The cost of these shows and buildings cannot be assessed, but other disbursements may easily have exceeded 800 millions.

The urban plebs benefited not only from donatives but from the opportunities of employment given by the building programme. His generals, notably Agrippa, also spent lavishly on buildings (Suet., *Aug.* 29). The veterans were satisfied with land and gifts of money, but this time Augustus did not have to expropriate farmers without compensation, as he had done in 41/0. (Even now some partisans of Antony were turned out of their lands, but they were given or promised money or land overseas; see Dio LI, 4, 6). As triumvir, Augustus had imposed heavy financial burdens on Italy; now he could refuse freewill offerings. All this must have had an incalculable effect in winning the 'universal consent' of which he boasts in 34.1.

Later expenditure is fairly well spread throughout the reign; but note (i) substantial distributions in cash and grain in 24 and 23 (see 15,1), roughly coinciding with the modification of the constitutional settlement of 27; (ii) distributions in 11 BC, after he became *pontifex maximus* (15,1); (iii) distributions in 5 and 2 BC (15,2 and 4) and great shows in 2 BC (22–3); in these years he held the consulship in order to introduce his sons to official life (4,4 n.). His largesses seem usually to have a particular political explanation.

Augustus does not mention the legacies to the Roman plebs (43,500,000 sesterces) and to soldiers, 1,000 to each praetorian and 300 to each legionary, for which he provided in his will (Tac., *Ann.* I, 8; Suet., *Aug.* 101), which Tiberius as his heir was responsible for paying. These gifts were calculated to ensure the loyalty of people and soldiers to his adoptive son and to make Tiberius' accession the smoother.

How was Augustus able to spend so lavishly? He was of course the administrator of half the empire, and the revenues at least of the provinces entrusted to him were at his disposal. But he is not referring to these revenues. From them he had to make large disbursements, in particular to pay the troops; but he does not mention this regular expenditure; naturally he could have taken no credit for spending public moneys on public needs. In a few cases he specifies the source of his benefactions; they came from 'my own money' (15,1; 17,1), 'my own patrimony' (15,1; 17,2) or 'my own granary and patrimony' (18), or from 'the proceeds of booty' (15,1; 21,1; 21,2). The booty of war belonged to the commander, though he was expected either to distribute it or to spend it on state purposes. In 27 Augustus induced his generals who had earned

triumphs to rebuild all the Italian roads out of their own booty, except
for the Flaminian road, whose reconstruction he himself undertook (20,5;
Suet., *Aug.* 30; Dio LIII, 22, 1; EJ, 286), and presumably paid for out of
booty, though he does not mention booty in this connexion. Similarly he
does not say that the portico of Octavius was built from the booty of the
Dalmatian war (Dio, XLIX, 43, 8). Again, when he claims that he was the
first and only man to pay compensation for land assigned to veterans, he
cannot mean that compensation had never been paid before: it had,
under a law passed by Caesar in 59, but then the compensation had
come from public revenues. Augustus was unique in paying it out of his
own pocket. We may infer that in all cases, even when he does not make
the point explicitly, the benefactions Augustus records were from his
private wealth. This wealth was one source of his control over the state.

Augustus' great lavishness in 30–27 may be explained by the fact that
in 30 he laid his hands on Cleopatra's treasure, the reserve funds of the
Ptolemies, which he could treat as his booty. But his resources were always
great. His initial largesses in 44 and the cost of raising a private army (1,1)
were financed from property inherited from his father, and from loans
made by his friends. He must have enriched himself in the proscriptions
and confiscations of 42. Thereafter, a principal source of his wealth consisted of the legacies his friends, and indeed all prominent Romans,
thought fit to leave him. In his will he claimed that in the last twenty
years of his life, i.e. from 6 BC, he had received 1,400 millions in legacies,
most of which he spent in the service of the state, as he had spent his two
paternal inheritances and much else that had been bequeathed to him;
his heirs were only to get 150 millions (Suet., *Aug.* 101). Before 6 BC
he had been the heir, for instance, of his nephew, Marcellus, the last
scion of one of the greatest and probably one of the richest noble houses
at Rome, of Maecenas, and of Agrippa, who had acquired the whole of
the Gallipoli peninsula as a personal estate, to say nothing of other
properties. It may be added that Tiberius, a careful but not ungenerous
man, was able to accumulate 2,700 millions by his death in AD 37 (Suet.,
Caligula 37).

15. This chapter provides the best evidence we have for the number
of the free poor at Rome. The corn dole was normally restricted to adult
males. It was probably five *modii* a month, (about forty-four litres or just
under 1¼ bushels).[1] A single man perhaps needed no more than three
modii, but the ration was not enough for a family. Between 23 and 2 BC
Augustus cut down the number of authorized recipients from 250,000 to
200,000; how he did this we do not know; it must not be assumed that the
population had decreased. In 23 he gave the recipients a whole year's
supply at his own cost. Dio LV, 26,3 says that in AD 6 he gave the poor

---

[1] The *modius* of wheat weighed about 12½ English pounds.

as much grain as they were receiving from the state. This is not mentioned here, proof that this document was imperfectly brought up to date.

15,4. There were four sesterces to each *denarius*.

16. See notes on 3,3 and 15–24.

17,1. This shows that the public revenues did not always cover ordinary expenditure (cf. 18). The treasury was administered from 28 to 23 by two prefects who had been praetors, and thereafter by two praetors. Augustus, however, exercised supervision through his own freedmen and slaves which he could have justified by the treasury's dependence on his subsidies. Hence he could issue an annual financial statement, and at his death leave 'a summary account of the whole empire, showing how many soldiers were under the standards in each district, and how much money there was in the treasury, and in the (provincial and departmental) chests, and how much was due to come in from the taxes; he added the names of the freedmen and slaves from whom accounts could be required' (Suet., *Aug.* 101). He was following the precedent of republican senators who had used their own freedmen and slaves for public administration; for instance, Quintus Cicero, as proconsul of Asia, had leant heavily on his freedman, Statius (Cic., *ad Qu. fr.* I, 2).

17,2. Until AD 6 Augustus had rewarded discharged soldiers out of his own wealth (3,3 with note). Now a new military treasury was set up to pay such rewards. (Dio LV, 24, 9 wrongly thought that the soldiers' wages also came from it.) It was administered by prefects who had held the praetorship. It was to be fed by (i) a 5% death duty on the estates of Roman citizens, except those of the very poor or those that were left to near kin, and (ii) a 1% tax on sales of goods by auction. The first was collected by tax-farmers, the second by the auctioneers. To put the treasury in funds at once, Augustus paid in a sum which would have provided rewards for about 14,000 men; the legionary was entitled to 12,000 sesterces on discharge. Dio LV, 25, 3 adds that he promised annual contributions and obtained gifts from client kings and from cities. Nothing here of the former: perhaps in the event Augustus paid none, or perhaps this is another case of the *Res Gestae* being not brought up to date.

The new system was introduced 'on Augustus' advice'. Dio says that he invited proposals from senators but selected the death-duties as the best means of raising revenue. They were found burdensome; since 167 BC citizens had paid no direct taxes on property in Italy except in emergencies. In AD 13 Augustus again asked for alternative schemes and himself suggested a land tax; this was disliked even more, and the death-duties became permanent (Dio LVI, 28, 4ff.). The story well illustrates

Augustus' desire to carry senatorial opinion with him and his success in getting his own way, in other words his use of *auctoritas* (pp. 84f.; 34,3 n.).

18. See note on 17,1.

19–21. 'The city was not adorned in proportion to the greatness of the empire and was subject to floods and fires: Augustus so beautified it that he justly boasted that he had found it made of brick and left it made of marble' (Suet., *Aug.* 28). See E. Strong, *CAH* X, 570ff. for details. The list Augustus gives of his chief buildings is intended not only to illustrate his liberality but to commemorate for posterity that *he* was the builder of so many fine monuments; as many were temples, it also confirms his claim to the virtue of 'piety' (34,2).

19. Of the buildings named here the senate house with its annexe, the Chalcidicum, and the temples of Apollo and Julius, were dedicated in 29–8, though begun earlier; the portico of Octavius (built in 167) was reconstructed in 33; the temple of Jupiter the Thunderer was dedicated in 22, those of Quirinus and Minerva in 16, and that of Juno before 17. Other dates are not known. On the temple of Apollo, see 21,2 n. He vowed the temple to Jupiter the Thunderer when he 'miraculously' escaped death by lightning in Spain in 26/5 (Suet., *Aug.* 29).

The Lupercal was a grotto in the Palatine, where sacrifices were offered in memory of the suckling of Romulus and Remus by the she-wolf. The *pulvinar* was a kind of box from which Augustus watched races in the circus; the word occurs in another sense in 9.2.

20,1. By the Capitol Augustus means the great temple of Jupiter, Juno and Minerva on that hill; it had been burned down in 9 BC. By not replacing the great Pompey's name with his own Augustus refused to condemn the memory of his father's rival, who in the eyes of some had stood for the Republic, as Augustus pretended to do. The date of these works is unknown.

20,2. Before Augustus, Rome was supplied with water by the Appian aqueduct built in 312 BC, the Old Anio aqueduct (273–271), the Marcian (143) and the Tepulan (125). As aedile in 33, Agrippa built the Julian (named in Augustus' honour); he continued to administer the water-supply without official title, and added the Virgo aqueduct in 19. After his death in 12 BC, Augustus took over the administration through sena-torial curators whom he appointed; he carried out the works mentioned here by 5/4 BC; he also built a new aqueduct, Alsietina, whose water was not fit for drinking. The net result of the new works from 33 onwards was perhaps to increase the supply of water by about 75%. As the city population must have grown enormously since 125, it can be assumed that by 33 the supply had come to be grossly inadequate. For the welfare of the inhabitants these measures were second only in importance to the improvements in the corn-supply.

20,3. 'My sons' are Gaius and Lucius Caesar (14,1 n.). Augustus began this work in AD 12 and probably did not live to complete it.

20,4. Before this work of restoration Horace wrote (*Odes* III, 6):

> 'Delicta maiorum immeritus lues,
> Romane, donec templa refeceris
>   aedesque labentis deorum et
>   foeda nigro simulacra fumo.
>
> dis te minorem quod geris, imperas:
> hinc omne principium, huc refer exitum:
>   di multa neglecti dederunt
>   Hesperiae mala luctuosae.'

'You will pay, Romans, through no fault of yours for the sins of your ancestors, until you have restored the temples and crumbling houses of the gods, and their images marred by the black filth of incense. By humbling yourselves before the gods you rule; with the gods all things begin, and they bring all to an end; neglect of the gods has brought much evil and suffering to Italy.'

This was a traditional Roman view, which was probably widely shared, whether or not Horace or Augustus himself held it; as 'the founder and restorer of all the temples', (Livy IV, 20), Augustus had a better chance of making men have faith in the end of civil wars and in the stability of the empire and his own régime.

20,5. At the same time generals of Augustus had to repair the other highways out of their booty (pp. 58f.).

21,1. Augustus vowed the temple of Mars the Avenger in 42 to celebrate the retribution exacted from Caesar's assassins. It stood in the Forum of Augustus. Both were completed in 2 BC and celebrated by games. Suetonius (*Aug.* 56) says that the Forum was less spacious than had been planned because Augustus would not expropriate the owners of adjoining land who were not willing to sell. The Forum was built to accommodate the increasing number of lawsuits (*ibid.* 29). The theatre of Marcellus was finished in 11 BC. All these were among Augustus' more splendid buildings (Suet., *Aug.* 29). M. Claudius Marcellus was the son of Augustus' sister, Octavia, by her first marriage; she later married Antony. Marcellus was the first husband of Augustus' only child, Julia, and was then probably intended to be Augustus' heir and successor, but died prematurely in 23 BC (cf. Virgil, *Aen.* VI, 860ff.).

21,2. Augustus placed his offerings in the Capitoline temple of Jupiter, the tutelary god of Rome, and in the temples of gods with whom he had a special connexion, his own deified father, Apollo, Vesta and Mars the

Avenger. For Mars see last note. Apollo he had chosen to regard as the god who gave him protection (see L. R. Taylor, *Divinity of the Roman Emperor*, pp. 118ff.; 131–4; 139f.); the victory at Actium was ascribed to Apollo's intervention (*Aen.* VIII, 704–6) and celebrated by games in Greece held every four years in Apollo's honour; and in 28 Octavian built a magnificent temple to Apollo on the Palatine (19,1), of solid and brilliantly white marble (*Aen.* VI, 69; VIII, 720), in which the colossal statue of the god bore his own features (Taylor, *op. cit.*, pp. 153f.); porticoes containing a public library were annexes of the temple, and quinquennial games for Apollo were inaugurated at Rome too. Augustus' special relation to Vesta dates from his assumption of the chief pontificate in 12 BC (11–12 n.). Suetonius (*Aug.* 30) says that the offerings made in the temple of Jupiter alone amounted to 16,000 lb. of gold (= 67,000,000 sesterces) and gems valued at 50,000,000 sesterces, a total exceeding that which Augustus claims for all the temples. But presumably Augustus would not have underestimated the sum, and Suetonius must be wrong.

21,3. *Aurum coronarium* is literally 'gold for crowns'. It was an ancient oriental custom for subjects to make gifts of gold to rulers or conquerors (e.g. II *Kings* 16, 8: 'Ahaz took the silver and gold that was found in the house of the Lord, and in the treasures of the king's house, and sent it for a present to the king of Assyria'); from the time of Alexander we find such gold made up into crowns, and from the second century Roman generals received such gifts in the East; they were not always voluntary. The practice of making the gold into crowns is probably Greek; at the Olympic and other great games victors originally received crowns of bay leaves, in the Roman period crowns of gold. It spread to Italy in the late Republic, perhaps not earlier than 47 BC, when Caesar exacted 'crown money' to help pay for his heavy expenses in civil war (Dio XLII, 50, 2). Lucius Antonius, who received a crown from each of the thirty-five Roman tribes in 41 when he triumphed for petty successes in the Alps, boasted that Marius had hardly any crowns for his great victories over the Cimbri and Teutones in 102/1 (*id.* XLVIII, 4, 6); perhaps he had none from citizens. In 29 and later Augustus remitted what had evidently become an impost in Italy. Provincials, however, still had to pay, just as they, and not Italy, paid direct taxes. (One lb. of gold = 4200 sesterces.)

The term 'colonies and *municipia*' often stands, as here, for the towns in Italy, though towns of both kinds are also found in the provinces. Colonies were towns in which the state settled Roman citizens; by Augustus' time the majority were towns which already existed, in which veterans were settled who lived side by side with the former inhabitants. All other towns of Roman citizens were *municipia*. The colonies had a more honorific status, but all the Italian towns equally enjoyed considerable powers of local self-government.

22,1.   Augustus adopted as his sons in 17 BC Gaius and Lucius Caesar, and in AD 4 Agrippa Postumus (Suet., *Aug.* 65); they were the sons of his daughter, Julia, and of Agrippa. He also adopted in AD 4 Tiberius Claudius Nero, the son of his wife, Livia, by her first marriage. His grandsons were Tiberius' own son, the younger Drusus, and Germanicus, the son of Tiberius' brother, the elder Drusus, whom Tiberius was made to adopt in AD 4 (Dio LV, 13, 2) (cf. 14,1 n.). These games are attested in 29, 28, 16, 12, 7 and 2 BC and in AD 6; one occasion to which Augustus alludes is undatable; likewise other shows he mentions.

In 22 BC Augustus limited to 100 the number of gladiators whom the praetors could produce in their shows; he reserved to himself the right to give gladiatorial exhibitions on a scale more than ten times greater. The fact that Augustus was keen on all forms of games and theatrical shows was commented on by Suetonius (*Aug.* 45); he refers to his 'eagerness as a spectator, and the pleasure he derived, which he never attempted to hide, and often admitted frankly'. He gave special prizes, and presents to actors, and 'he watched with the greatest enthusiasm boxing matches, particularly when the fighters were Italians, and not only organized matches . . . but also brawls between gangs of toughs in narrow streets in the city. In summary, he honoured all types of professional entertainers by his interest in them.' Suetonius goes on to notice the fact that he preserved and increased the privileges of athletes, insisted on the possibility of gladiators being spared, and gave extra protection to actors, who had previously been subject to arbitrary punishment by the magistrates. Tacitus (*Ann.* I, 77, 3) refers to the fact that Augustus had decreed that stage players should be exempt from corporal punishment.

22,2.   The shows here were theatrical productions and chariot races.

The Secular Games of 17 BC were the greatest religious festival of Augustus' reign and the best documented of any in Roman history, see Warde Fowler, *Religious Experience of the Roman People*, pp. 439ff. They take their name from the Latin *saeculum*, a period representing the longest stretch of a man's life. They were to be celebrated only once in such a period. The first certainly historic occasion was in the crisis of the first war with Carthage in 249 BC, and the second in 149. The period implied is 100 years, but Augustus took the view that it was properly 110 years, and held that they were due in 17, on what reckoning is not clear. His real object was certainly to symbolize the inauguration of a new and golden age in Rome's history, such as Virgil had predicted in his fourth eclogue, written in 40, and again in *Aeneid* I, 278–96, where Jupiter declares that with the birth of 'Caesar', 'who is to make the Ocean the bound of empire and the stars the bound of his fame' an age of universal peace under Rome's world-wide dominion will begin; 'with wars laid to rest the harsh ages (*saecula*) shall grow mild'; it is manifest that Augustus, not Julius, is meant by 'Caesar', since the birth of Julius had not brought in an era of peace.

The form of the festival was prescribed by a Sibylline oracle, doubtless invented for the occasion, which has been preserved together with long fragments of the senate's decree by which the festival was regulated and of the official record of the proceedings; see further E. Fraenkel, *Horace*, pp. 364ff., with full references. For the occasion, Horace wrote the *Carmen Saeculare* to be sung by boys and girls chosen from among those whose parents were both alive. It gives expression to the underlying ideas of the festival. The poet prays that the Sun may never look on anything greater than the city of Rome, that the goddess of childbirth may prosper the decisions of the senate, embodied in Augustus' contemporary marriage law (cf. 6,2) and designed to stimulate the birth-rate among the upper classes, that fertility may be granted to crops and flocks, that the gods may make the young learn to be upright and give their elders a peaceful old age; and he acclaims the revival of Rome's prestige— Medes and Albanians, Indians and Scythians stand in awe of her—and the restoration of peace, plenty and of the traditional virtues of Romans. All this is hardly poetical, but it illustrates what were considered at the time the greatest achievements of the new régime: (i) the diplomatic victory over the Parthians in 20 (cf. 27,2; 29,2; 32,2); (ii) in general, the establishment of peace and the resulting growth of prosperity (cf. 13 n.); (iii) the contemporary measures by which Augustus was seeking to revive the old morality and to induce the upper classes to increase and multiply (6,2 n.; 8,5 n.); (iv) the new veneration for the old Roman religion (cf. 7,3 n.; 19–20).

Augustus presided over the festival as chairman of the quindecimvirs (7,3 n.). Agrippa, who also belonged to that priestly college, was now his son-in-law and partner in the tribunician power (p. 47) and in that capacity was associated with him in the celebrations.

The institution of the new games of Mars in 2 BC (cf. 21,1 n.) again shows Augustus seeking to win the hearts of the urban population of Rome by lavish shows, as well as by his distributions of grain and money and by his building programme, which must have provided many of the poor with jobs.

22,3. Such 'hunts' are attested in 11 and 2 BC and AD 12; on one occasion 260 lions and thirty-six crocodiles were killed. Gibbon's *Decline and Fall*, chapter IV (I, pp. 93f. ed. Bury) has a glowing and ironical description of such a 'hunt'.

23. This 'sea-battle', staged at huge cost in 2 BC, was a special kind of gladiatorial show. Caesar had given one, and Claudius gave another, on a still greater scale, described by Tacitus, *Ann.* XII, 56f. and Suetonius, *Claudius* 21.

24,1. This is the only instance where Augustus records an act bene-
ficial to the provinces. Probably he mentions it only as an illustration of
his piety (cf. 34,2). The opponent to whom he alludes is Antony.

An important inscription from Cyme in Asia, published by H. W.
Pleket, *Greek Inscriptions in the Rijksmuseum van Oudheden at Leyden*,
1958, pp. 49ff., is relevant. It gives the text of an order issued by Augustus
and Agrippa in 27 as consuls, and reads: 'In regard to public or sacred
places in cities or in the territory of a city in every province or to offerings
dedicated in such places, no one is to remove them or buy them or take
them from any one as a gift; if any have been removed or bought or
received as gifts, whoever is in charge of the province is to provide for
their restoration to the public or sacred place of the city. . . .' This text,
preserved in Greek, the end of which is fragmentary, is followed on the
stone by the record in Latin of a decision by a proconsul of Asia, taken in
accordance with the 'order' (*iussum*) of Augustus; though he ignores
Agrippa, he cannot be referring to anything but the immediately preceding instructions. This illustrates Augustus' right as consul to inter-
vene in senatorial provinces (cf. Jones, chapter 1, and below, p. 83).

25,1. Augustus alludes to his victory over Sextus Pompey in 36. Son
of the great Pompey, Sextus controlled the western Mediterranean sea
and Sicily from 42 to 36, and for a time Sardinia, and in 39 was recognized virtually as a partner in the empire by the triumvirs. See e.g. Rice
Holmes, pp. 81; 106–16. His fleets were largely manned by slaves, and
of those Augustus captured he crucified 6,000 and handed the rest back
to their masters. But it was mere propaganda to treat the war as one
against pirates and slaves (cf. 27,3); Sextus enjoyed the support of many
eminent Republicans, and if not a sincere Republican himself, was aiming
at personal power, just like the triumvirs.

Sextus' defeat was of great moment for Octavian. It gave him the
opportunity to eliminate Lepidus as well as Sextus, to get control of many
more legions, and of Africa in addition to Sicily and Sardinia. As a result
he could put an end to the famine, endemic in Rome so long as Sextus
could cut off supplies from these provinces, which were the principal
sources of grain imports. More than all this, he could now earn golden
opinions in Italy, discharging soldiers, remitting taxes and proclaiming
that civil wars were at an end. A monument at Rome declared that 'peace,
long disturbed, he re-established on land and sea' (Appian, *BC* V, 130).
From this time he began to win the good-will of all Italy (Syme, chapter
XVII).

Augustus does not draw attention to these political consequences of his
victory. But his claim to have made the sea peaceful has overtones which
cannot be restricted to the year 36 and of which he was probably con-
scious. Later, by establishing permanent fleets at Misenum, Ravenna

and elsewhere in the Mediterranean, he prevented the recrudescence of piracy and made the sea safer for trade. This achievement was often celebrated, e.g. by Horace (*Odes* IV, 5, 19); *Pacatum volitant per mare nautae* ('Sailors fly across the peaceful sea'), cf. Suet., *Aug.* 98, 2 quoted in 13 n.

25,2. On this see Syme, chapter XX. Dio L, 3, 3ff. records that on information brought by M. Titius and L. Munatius Plancus Octavian seized and published Antony's will; the terms so incensed senate and people that war was declared on Cleopatra, and Antony was divested of all official power; it was expected that Antony would make himself a public enemy (*hostis*) by taking her side, but he was not yet declared to be such (Suet., *Aug.* 17, 2, who asserts the opposite, may refer to a later occasion), though Octavian announced his personal enmity (*inimicitia*) towards him. The date must be summer 32. Dio L, 6, 2ff. then summarizes the military preparations on both sides, stating that Octavian had the support of Italy, the western provinces and Illyricum, Antony of the East, and that both leaders bound 'the alliances' to themselves by oaths. He adds that Octavian won over Antony's partisans in Italy by menaces or favours. Suet., *Aug.* 17, 2 also refers to an oath of this time, which Antony's clients in Bononia were excused from taking. Both evidently refer to the oath mentioned in the text and Suetonius implies that it was not quite so voluntary as Augustus makes out.

Dio LVII, 3, 2 says that on Augustus' death the Italians took the same oath to Tiberius as they had taken to Augustus; this must be the oath of allegiance (*in verba*) taken at Rome by the consuls, leading equestrian officials, senate, soldiers and people immediately after Augustus' death, and later in Gaul (Tac., *Ann.* I, 7; 34). Such an oath was taken in Rome and the provinces to each emperor on his accession, and from AD 38 was renewed annually. As it was taken by civilians as well as soldiers, it cannot be the military oath (also *in verba*) which bound soldiers to obey commands and not desert the standards. Its nature can be determined from several inscriptions which contain the formulae of oaths taken (a) by resident Romans and natives at Gangra in Paphlagonia in 3 BC, shortly after it was incorporated in the province of Galatia (EJ, 315); (b) by Cypriots on the accession of Tiberius (*JRS* L (1960), 75ff.); (c) in Portugal, Asia and perhaps Italy in AD 38 on the accession of Caligula (Syme, p. 288 n. 3, where read *SIG*, not *OGIS* 797). We translate (a):

'I swear by Zeus, Ge, Helios, and all gods and goddesses and by Augustus himself that I will be loyal to Caesar Augustus and to his children and descendants all the days of my life in word, deed and mind, accounting as friends whomsoever they account as friends and regarding as personal enemies (ἐχθροί) whomsoever they judge to be such, and that on their behalf I will spare neither spirit nor life nor children, but that in every way I will endure every danger in their interest. Whatsoever I may learn or hear that is said or planned or done adverse to them, that I will reveal, and I will be a personal enemy of any one who says, plans or does any such thing. Whomsoever they judge to be their personal enemies, them I will pursue and resist by land and sea with arms and iron. But if I should infringe this oath or not act in accordance with its terms, I invoke on myself and on my body, spirit, life, children and my whole race and interest utter and total destruction down to the last of my line and all who descend from me, and may the bodies of my family or issue not be received by land or sea nor enjoy their fruits.'

The substance of this oath is very similar to that of the other oaths; though the formulation varies greatly, different gods are invoked, and in some cases the emperor's descendants are mentioned only vaguely as 'his house', or not at all.

The terms are not appropriate to the powerless inhabitants of Paphlagonia nor to the internal peace that then prevailed, nor again to conditions at the accession of Tiberius or Caligula. But they are appropriate to the situation in 32 BC, when Octavian had become a *personal* enemy of Antony and wished to lead all Italy in a war against him. It may be inferred, then, that such an oath, with local variations in the formula, was taken in Italy and the west in 32, after Antony's defeat in the east, in other regions on annexation (e.g. Paphlagonia), and everywhere on the accession of new emperors.

The oath-takers are bound to an individual, not to a magistrate of the Roman people. The oath is extra-constitutional. In AD 14 it was taken to Tiberius before the senate had even met to discuss and confirm his constitutional powers. The oath of 32 did not, then, confer any legal power on Octavian. Nor did the demand that he should be 'leader'. Legally, a military command could be conferred only by the duly constituted assembly at Rome; see G. E. F. Chilver, *Historia* I (1950), pp. 408ff. Augustus is describing a popular demonstration in his favour which had great moral effect, which *helps* to explain his claim in 34,1 that he enjoyed universal consent, and which bound Italy etc. to him by a *religious* tie. It is hard to say how far men were in practice influenced by the sanctity of oaths.

25,3. The senate at this time numbered about 1,000. Some senators had long been with Antony, and many others fled to him in 32 along with both the consuls (Dio L, 2, 6f.). It cannot, however, be inferred that if over 700 senators were with Octavian, 300 were with Antony, nor safely insinuated that Octavian took all 700 senators with him because he could not trust them if they remained behind. The presence of so many senators, the true representatives of Italy, may have been desired principally because it gave colour to Octavian's claim that he stood for Italy against the renegade Roman, Antony. See Virgil, *Aen*. VIII, 678ff.: 'on one side Caesar Augustus leading the Italians to battle, with *senate* and people, the gods of household and state . . .; on the other Antony with his barbarian wealth and motley panoply, victorious from the peoples of the dawn and the shore of the Red Sea, brings with him Egypt and the might of the East and the remote Bactrians; in his train, a sinful sight, his Egyptian paramour'.

26–33. *Augustus' successes over foreign peoples*

Augustus records in these chapters the more outstanding military and diplomatic achievements of his reign. Contemporary poets expressed the hope or belief that he could bring the whole world under Roman rule (see, for instance, the prediction of Jupiter in *Aeneid* I, 278–96); in 13 BC Horace claimed that 'the fame and majesty of the empire had been extended to the rising of the sun from its western couch' and that 'neither those who drink the deep waters of the Danube will break the Julian commands nor the Getae, neither the Chinese and faithless Persians, nor those born near the river Don (*Odes* IV, 15). It is generally believed that Augustus had no ambition to fulfil the ambitions which Horace hyperbolically represents as already achieved, but that his object from the first was to provide the empire with more easily defensible frontiers, an object in which he succeeded (cf. Tac., *Ann*. I, 9); see J. G. C. Anderson in *CAH* X, pp. 254–65 and R. Syme, *ibid*., pp. 340–2; 351–5. For a heretical view that, after completing internal pacification and allowing time for the empire to rest after prolonged civil wars, Augustus did embark on a cautious but systematic programme of world conquest, which was frustrated by the revolts in Pannonia and Germany in AD 6 and 9, and that only at the end of his life did he fall back on the policy of keeping the empire within its then existing limits (Tac., *Ann*. I, 11), see Brunt, *JRS* LIII (1963), 170–6.

Whatever be held about Augustus' ultimate aims, it is beyond question that he was a great conqueror; he added to the empire Egypt, a great part of the Balkan peninsula (modern Bulgaria, most of Jugoslavia and part of Hungary), modern Austria, Switzerland and part of Bavaria, and before AD 6–9 he was bent on annexing Bohemia, and Germany at least west of the Elbe. It is also clear that naturally enough he regarded his success abroad, including diplomatic victories, as among his most memorable achievements; the stress he lays on them in these chapters shows that he wished to be remembered for them and suggests that they were in his view important in winning over public opinion to the new régime. Suetonius says that he had no desire to increase the empire or his glory in war (*Aug*. 21), but his own acts and words suggest that Suetonius wrongly saw Augustus as a precursor of Hadrian, under whom he wrote. Augustus was the 'good' emperor *par excellence*; hence his authority was naturally invoked to sanction the policy of his successors, such as Hadrian. It was characteristic of Augustus that he set up in his new forum statues of those who had triumphed in the past and had 'raised the power of the Roman people from insignificance to the greatest might' and explained in a proclamation that he had done this in order that the citizens might expect him and later *principes* to emulate their example (Suet., *Aug.* 31).

Details of the campaigns or diplomacy to which Augustus refers will be found in *CAH* X, chapters IX and XII (by R. Syme and J. G. C. Anderson).

26,1. This vague and grandiloquent statement could not easily have been checked by readers. Gagé thinks that, apart from the northern provinces, Augustus had in mind the annexation of Galatia, bordering on Asia (25 BC), and of Judaea, bordering on Syria (AD 6). Perhaps he had. Yet from another point of view Augustus could call vassal kingdoms (like Galatia and Judaea) 'members and parts of the empire' (Suet., *Aug.* 48); on this conception the empire was not extended when they were brought under direct Roman administration, instead of being indirectly under Roman control.

26,2. There were campaigns in Gaul, 27–25 BC; in Spain, 27–19 BC (cf. 13 n.); in Germany, especially 12–6 BC. Velleius (II, 97) says that by 6 BC Germany west of the Elbe had been reduced almost to a tributary province; by AD 9, on the eve of revolt, the legate, P. Quinctilius Varus, was trying cases and seeking to levy tribute and found colonies (Vell. II, 117; Tac., *Ann.* I, 59; Dio LVI, 18, 4; Florus II, 30, 31) and there was a provincial cult of Rome and Augustus (*Ann.* I, 57). By then it must have been regarded as a province, though its loss was accepted after Varus' defeat; subsequent campaigns were intended only to retrieve Roman reputation (*Ann.* I, 3, 6; 11, 4). Here it is not called a province, unlike Gaul and Spain; perhaps the phraseology was altered after AD 9, or the words were written soon after 6 BC, before formal annexation had been decided on. Clearly, Augustus would hardly have claimed the pacification of Germany in just these terms if he had been writing after Varus' defeat, and the second view seems preferable. See Addenda, p. 82.

26,3. The pacification of the Alpine tribes was achieved in a series of campaigns from 35 to 7/6 and then commemorated by a monument in the Maritime Alps, set up to Augustus 'because under his leadership and auspices all the Alpine tribes from the upper to the lower sea had been brought under the rule of the Roman people' (EJ, 40). This made a most valuable contribution to the security of the inhabitants of north Italy; for the serious depredations of Alpine peoples before this time see Strabo IV, 205–6; V, 213; Dio XLIX, 34, 2; LIV, 22.

Augustus' claim to have not made war unjustly on these peoples is extended by Suetonius (*Aug.* 21), who says that 'he made no war on any people without just and necessary reasons'. That had always been the Roman way by their own account, but they made themselves judges in their own cause. The Alpine peoples subdued by Augustus included the Salassi, most of whom were sold into slavery (Dio LIII, 25, 4 but cf. EJ, 338). They had levied tolls on travellers over the pass they controlled. The Romans called this brigandage (Strabo IV, 205), but they levied tolls themselves in the Alpine passes; cf. also 26,5 n.

26,4. The voyage was in 5 BC; the peoples concerned lived near the mouth of the Elbe and in Jutland. See Addenda, p. 82.

26,5. The Ethiopian expedition was in 24–22 and the Arabian in 25–24. Strabo, who accompanied the second expedition, says that Augustus intended to win over the Sabaeans or to subdue them (XVI, 780). An invasion was an odd way of winning their friendship. It seems clear that the expedition was a naked piece of imperialism; Augustus desired to lay hands himself on the large revenues accruing from the heavy tolls charged by the Sabaeans on the spice trade, or to reduce the heavy loss of gold and silver which the trade entailed for the empire (Pliny, *Nat. Hist.* VI, 162; XII, 84; Strabo XVI, 780). The Arabian expedition failed in any such aim, but Strabo (XVI, 779) claims that the Sabaeans became vassals of Rome; we may think of some empty form of homage. The Ethiopians too sent ambassadors to Augustus in 21/0, and may have been regarded as vassals. See *CAH* X, pp. 239–53.

27,1. The statement that Egypt was brought under the power of the Roman people (30 BC) is also found in other Augustan documents (EJ, 14; 37). The state domains and the peasants who worked them, previously called 'royal', now became in name 'public' (H. I. Bell, *CAH* X, pp. 292f.). The taxes belonged to the *aerarium*, the Roman state treasury (Velleius, II, 39). But though Egypt was undoubtedly a province (*ibid.* 284f.), Augustus and his successors were regarded by the natives as Pharaohs, and it was administered virtually as a private appanage of the emperor, through equestrian officials; senators were not allowed to set foot in it without imperial consent. The reasons given by Tacitus (*Ann.* II, 59; *Hist.* I, 11) and Dio (LI, 17, 1) were the fickleness and turbulence of the population, the importance of Egypt as a source of grain and the ease with which in the case of revolt it could be defended against invasion. These explanations are conjectural. Tacitus describes Augustus' special treatment of Egypt as one of the 'secrets of empire'; in other words, he did not know just why it was specially treated. Of course, Augustus himself does not even allude here to these arrangements; but

we need not tax him with deception; there was no reason why he should
have done so.

It seems possible that the main reason why Augustus excluded from
Egypt all senators, the class in whom the Republican tradition was most
alive, was the fact that in Egypt he had to rule in the ancient style, with
the attributes of the Hellenistic dynasty of the Ptolemies, or of the
Pharaohs (cf. H. I. Bell, *CAH* X, pp. 284f.) He had assailed Antony for
'going native' (Syme, pp. 273ff.), but his own position in Egypt was
much the same as Antony's.

27,2. Lucullus and Pompey had overrun Armenia, but Pompey recognized the Armenian king, Tigranes, as a vassal of Rome. After Artavasdes, Tigranes' son and successor, had betrayed him during his Parthian
campaign of 36, Antony deposed him in 34 and annexed the country.
Artavasdes' son, Artaxes, recovered the realm on Antony's fall but was
assassinated in 20; it was then that Augustus had his brother, Tigranes,
crowned as a vassal of Rome. 'The model set by our ancestors' seems to
be the action of Pompey. The coins proclaim the conquest or recovery of
Armenia; as a client kingdom, Augustus regarded it as within the
empire (cf. 26,1 n.), but preferred to control it indirectly. This policy was
hard to carry out, as it was not easy to find kings who were both loyal to
Rome and acceptable to their own people. Augustus here omits part of the
chequered history of Rome's relations with Armenia after 20, mentioning
only the installation of Ariobarzanes in AD 2 by Gauis and his later support of Tigranes IV perhaps in AD 6. The description of Tiberius as 'then
my stepson', i.e. in 20 BC, implies that the text was revised in or after
AD 4. For a full account see Anderson, *CAH* X, chapter IX.

27,3. Augustus professes to regard all the provinces which had been
assigned to Antony by the pact of Brundisium in 40 (Syme, p. 217) as
lost to Rome by Antony's treason and recovered by himself. Antony had
in fact granted part of the province of Cilicia to the Galatian king,
Amyntas, and the coast to Cleopatra, who also received Cyprus, Cyrene
and part of Syria, districts previously under Roman provincial administration; in the 'donations of Alexandria' (34 BC) parts of the enlarged
kingdom of Egypt, together with the newly-annexed Armenia (see last
note), were distributed among the children Cleopatra had borne him. For
a favourable interpretation of Antony's policy see Syme, chapter XIX.
Sardinia and Sicily were recovered from Sextus Pompey (see 25,1 note).

28. Colonies were traditionally founded as 'bulwarks of empire'
(Cicero), and some of the Augustan colonies in the provinces served for
the protection of turbulent areas as well as for the settlement of veterans;
hence the reference to them in this military section of the *Res Gestae*.
The twenty-eight colonies in Italy doubtless include some founded in

41/0; they cannot all be identified with certainty, nor can we check the claim that all remained prosperous. See Addenda, p. 82.

29,1. Roman standards had been lost in Dalmatia in 48 BC and were regained in Octavian's Illyrian campaigns of 35/4. We do not know when standards were lost in Spain and Gaul; in Spain their recovery may have been in 25; the successes recorded must have been gained by generals fighting under Augustus' auspices (see 4,2 n.).

29,2. The Parthians captured Roman standards at Crassus' great defeat at Carrhae in 53, and from Decidius Saxa in 40 and Antony in 36. As a result of negotiations they were restored in 20, when Augustus also imposed a king on Armenia (27,2). This great diplomatic success, for which he was offered a triumph, was endlessly celebrated by poets and on coins. Here Augustus represents the Parthians as suppliants for Roman friendship (cf. 32,2); the term often meant 'vassalage', and 'suppliants' shows that Augustus meant his readers to think that the Parthian king had become a vassal of Rome: the reality was different. By placing the recovered standards in 2 BC in the temple of Mars the Avenger (21,1 n.), Augustus made it appear that the god through his agency had avenged a disgrace to the Roman people as well as the assassination of his adoptive father.

30. Augustus refers to the original conquest of Pannonia in 12–9 BC by Tiberius 'who was then my stepson'; the phrase indicates revision in or after AD 4 when he adopted Tiberius. See Syme, *CAH* X, pp. 355ff. He ignores Tiberius' suppression of the great Pannonian revolt in AD 6–9, one indication that his work was not fully brought up to date (p. 6). In section 1 he stresses the unprecedented character of Tiberius' success; section 2 adds to the effect: 'my armies actually crossed the Danube'. Various occasions are known, in 29 BC (*CAH* X, pp. 116ff.) and more than one between 6 BC and AD 4 (*ibid.*, 365–7). Strabo, a contemporary, regards the Dacians as almost subjects of Rome (VII, 305). This was an exaggeration, which Augustus' language was calculated to foster.

In 12–9 BC Tiberius was still a legate fighting under Augustus' auspices (4,2 n.); however, he was allowed an ovation in 9 BC and a triumph in 7 for victories in Germany and shared an imperatorial salutation with Augustus as early as 9 (Dio LIV, 33, 5; LV, 2, 4; 8, 2; Vell. II, 96–7; Valerius Maximus V, 5, 3; Suet., *Tib.* 9); *either* Tiberius received an independent grant of *imperium*, *or* he was specially privileged, as Augustus' stepson, to receive honours normally denied to legates.

31,1. Again Augustus brings out the uniqueness of his achievements. There was a valuable trade with India through Egypt and Arabia and silks were even brought by caravan·from China (cf. M. P. Charlesworth, *Trade Routes and Commerce of the Roman Empire*, chapters 4 and 6),

Indian embassies are attested in 25 and 20. Horace in 17 said that 'now the Scythians and proud Indians seek rulings' from Rome (*Carmen Saeculare*, 55f.), compare his allusion to the Chinese, cited on p. 69.

31,2. Bastarnae and Scythians lived beyond the Danube and their petition of 'friendship' (cf. 29,2 n.; 31,1 n.), like that of the Sarmatians reflects the success of the expeditions across the Danube (cf. 30). The Albani lived in the Caucasus, the Hiberi in Georgia. On the King of Media, which adjoined Armenia to the East, see 32,1 n.

32,1. Tiridates was a pretender to the Parthian throne who fled to Augustus in 29; Augustus declined to support his claims, but also in 20 refused to surrender him to King Phraates. The younger Phraates came into Augustus' power *c.* 25 and may have been recognized as king, but was given back to his father in the settlement of 20 (29,2 n.). The Median Artavasdes, father of Tigranes, whom Augustus put on the Armenian throne in 20, came to him after Actium; he had taken the Roman side against Parthia, supporting Antony, and Augustus made him ruler of Armenia Minor. Nothing is known of the King of Adiabene (beyond the Tigris). Nor do we know the circumstances in which British princes fled to Augustus. Augustus was often adjured to resume the conquest of Britain but deferred it, in the end indefinitely (Tac., *Agricola* 13), and Strabo (IV, 200) attests that the British kings sent embassies and sought Roman 'friendship'; in the official view they had virtually made the island Roman. No such embassies are mentioned in 31, where Augustus confines himself to naming embassies from peoples not previously 'friendly' to Rome; the Britons did not come in this category, as princes in south-east Britain had become nominally vassals of Rome in 54 BC, though they soon defaulted in payment of tribute. Strabo's *embassies* must surely be distinct from the arrival of *refugee* princes at Augustus' court. Dumnobellaunus and Tincommius are known from British coins.

Maelo is named by Strabo as the Sugambrian chief hostile to Rome. It is not clear in what relation his flight to Augustus stands to the success Tiberius obtained in 8 BC in capturing 40,000 Sugambri and settling them west of the Rhine (*CAH* X, p. 363; Suet., *Tib.*, 9).

The Marcomanni moved under Roman pressure from the Main valley, *c.* 9 BC to Bohemia, where their chief, Maroboduus, established a formidable kingdom (cf. Tac., *Ann.* II, 63); the Roman plan of subduing it in AD 6 was frustrated by the revolt in Pannonia and Dalmatia (*CAH* X, 364ff.). The name of the refugee king and the circumstances of his flight are unknown.

32,2. King Phraates IV sent his four legitimate sons to Augustus, *c.* 10 BC, to get them out of the way, in order that his bastard son, Phraataces, might succeed. Two died at Rome. Phraataces, who succeeded in 2 BC after murdering his father, demanded the return of his half-brothers, which Augustus refused. Only after the fall of Phraataces did he send back one of the brothers, Vonones, when the Parthians wished to make him king in c. AD 6 (cf. 33). Vonones, who had been Romanized, could not win the loyalty of his subjects and was expelled c. AD 11–12; he tried to make himself king in Armenia, but without success; interned by the Romans, he escaped and was put to death in 19. The last of the four brothers, Phraates, was encouraged by Rome in an attempt to secure the Parthian crown in AD 35, but fell ill and died.

32,3. Once more Augustus insists on the unprecedented character of the contacts he established with foreign peoples, among whom he no doubt had in mind here the Ethiopians and Arabians.

33. On Vonones see 32,2 and note. Ariobarzanes, made king of Media in the eastern settlement of 20, subsequently became king of Armenia (27,2n.). Augustus insinuates that the Medes and Parthians were virtually his subjects.

34,1. Augustus states that before 28/7 he was in complete control of the state and that he then surrendered it to the senate and people. He does not say what action they took or what powers they then accorded to him. His statements are therefore not useful for determining his constitutional position after 27, on which see p. 9, but they are relevant to (a) the time-table of surrender and (b) his position before the surrender.

(a) The surrender took place in 28 as well as 27. Dio (LIII, 1–2) says that in 28 (i) he allowed his colleague in the consulship, Agrippa, to alternate with him in having the *fasces*; (ii) that he took the customary oath on laying down the office at the end of the year; (iii) that he abolished illegal and unjust regulations of the triumvirate, setting the end of the year as the time for their expiration. (Other events recorded have no constitutional bearings.) It follows from (i) that until 28 Octavian had denied equal power (symbolized by the *fasces*) to his colleagues in the consulship: this is also implied in 34,3 below. Dio's third statement has been ingeniously explained as meaning that citizens were given until 31 December, 28 to challenge rulings of the triumvirate; unless challenged, they would stand (E. W. Gray, *Gnomon* 1961, 193, citing Pliny, *Ep.* X 56 (64) on the effects of rescinding legal decisions). Consuls normally swore at the end of their year that they had taken no action contrary to the laws (Pliny, *Panegyric* 65); apparently 28 was the first year in which Octavian had not scrupled to take this oath. The end of 28 was, therefore, the end of a period in which he had presumably not been bound by the laws. Dio makes him restore the armies, laws and subject peoples in January 27 (LIII, 4), and other sources, quoted on p. 9, imply that previously he had controlled all the provinces, and that magistrates had not enjoyed their full powers; the statement of Suetonius (*Aug.* 40) that he revived the old rights of the electoral assemblies, presumably at this time, seems to show that they had not been freely elected. Augustus here asserts that he had been master of the state, and thus confirms the other sources.

(b) By what right had he been master? There are various views. (i) From 32 to January 27 he still acted as triumvir, dropping only the title, which was inapposite with the elimination of Antony and Lepidus (cf. 7.1 n.). (ii) He brought out the discretionary character of the *imperium* (p. 83) he held as consul from 31 to its full extent. This fails to explain the inferiority in which he placed his consular colleagues before 28. (iii) He had no legal warrant for absolute power, but relied only on force and 'universal consent'. (iv) He had a new legal grant of absolute power after the triumvirate expired. For this view some would invoke his statement here. The Latin words *potitus rerum omnium* are restored from the Greek, and the Greek participle corresponding to *potitus* is an aorist. It could then be rendered 'when I had secured complete control of affairs with universal consent', and the reference to universal consent taken to suggest a formal vote of absolute power. But no such grant is recorded in the years from 32 to 28, even by Dio, who loves to dwell on the honours then heaped on Octavian. Moreover the run of the clauses in the Latin sentence, which is certain, would place such a grant after the end of civil wars in 30 and still leave his position in 31 unaccounted for. It seems better, then, to suppose that Augustus is not concerned here with the legal basis of his power and is saying either that after crushing Antony he acquired absolute control *de facto* with all men's approval, or more probably that on the eve of the great surrender he was in complete control of the state; on the last view the participle *potitus* is a true perfect, misunderstood by the Greek translator. See also G. E. F. Chilver, *Historia* I (1950), pp. 408ff.

The constitutional puzzle is less important than Augustus' claim to 'universal consent'. Though *ex parte* and exaggerated, it may not be far from the truth. He had re-established peace and order (cf. 13 n.) and it was probably widely believed that he had saved Rome from eastern despotism (cf. 25,3 n.); the relief of Horace, for one, at the news of Cleopatra's death rings genuine (*Odes* I, 37). His munificence in 30–27 must have won him popularity (see 15–24 note., pp. 57 ff.). The oath taken to him in 32 (25,2 n.) surely betokened wide support, and since 32 he had acted in such a way as to win and not to forfeit men's good opinions. There is no need to think that he means that the universal consent which he claims was expressed in any single act. If *potitus* is a true perfect participle, the universal consent existed in 28/7, though it could have been built up and manifested in many ways over the preceding years.

Augustus does not say what new power the senate and people granted to him after the great surrender; for this see p. 9. His theme here is not his constitutional position, but the public recognition of his services. 34,1 leads on to 34,2—the tributes paid to his outstanding virtues—to 34,3, the pre-eminent influence he still enjoyed when he had ceased to exercise autocratic control, and to the grand climax of 35.

34,2. Suetonius describes the way in which Octavian received the name Augustus as follows (*Aug.* 7, 2): 'He assumed the *cognomen* of Augustus in accordance with the motion of Munatius Plancus. Some [senators] had voted that he ought to be called Romulus, since he too was a founder of the city, but the view carried the day that he should rather be named Augustus, a *cognomen* that was not only new but even grander, since places that are sacred or in which something is consecrated with augural rites are spoken of as 'august', whether from the augmentation [of their worth] (*auctu*) or from the way the birds moved or tasted food [as observed by the augurs] (*avium gestu gustuve*). This is also shown by the words of Ennius:

> "After famous Rome was founded by august augury"
> (*augusto augurio postquam inclyta condita Roma est*),

Dio (LIII, 16, 7–8) also says that Augustus was at first keen to be called Romulus, probably because it would for him have symbolized his claim to be the second founder of Rome; one may compare his receiving the title of 'father of his country' in 2 BC (35 with note). Dio adds that he gave the idea up because of the regal associations of Romulus. Perhaps too he remembered the legend that Romulus had been translated to Heaven by the daggers of the senators.

The name Augustus had, in fact, three nuances. (i) 'All the most precious or sacred things are termed *augusta*' says Dio (*loc. cit.*). Ovid equates the word with *sanctus* ('holy'). Livy applies it to the bodily form of Hercules, who was supposed to have become a god because of his services to mankind (I, 7, 9) and says of Decius (VIII, 9, 10): 'He was a little more august than a man to look at, as if he had been sent from Heaven'. It was appropriate to the 'son of the divine Julius', who was himself *sacrosanctus* or inviolable, who had already been hailed as a god or divinely sent saviour by Virgil (*Ecl.* I, 6; *Georg.* I, 498ff.) and who, according to Horace (*Odes* I, 2, 25ff.) was at least destined for Heaven. Augustus was not officially deified in his lifetime at Rome, though in many provinces he was, but he was assimilated to the gods in subtle ways; for instance, his birthday was a public holiday, i.e. a 'holy' day, and libations were offered to his Genius as early as 29: for this cult see 35 n. It is significant that the Greeks did not transliterate 'Augustus' as a name, but translated it as a title, and that its divine nuance in the name is brought out in the Greek word which rendered it, and which means 'worthy of reverence' (σεβαστός). (ii) Dio also says (LIII, 18, 2) that the name suggested the splendour of the emperor's ἀξίωμα, the word used in the Greek paraphrase to render *auctoritas* or 'influence' (34,3 with note); the same Greek word is used incidentally by Thucydides (II, 65, 8), an author whom Dio imitated, to denote one of the sources of Pericles' power. *Augustus* and *auctoritas*, in fact, come from the same root, and Suetonius in the passage quoted above shows that the connexion was felt. (iii) Suetonius also connects *augustus* with *augury*. Here he is wrong, but may reflect a contemporary view. The word certainly suggested the 'august augury' with which Romulus had founded Rome, that is to say the appearance of the twelve vultures whom Romulus had seen according to the legend and who, curiously enough, were also seen by Augustus when he became consul for the first time in 43 (Suet., *Aug.* 95). It thus connected him with Romulus, not as king, but as the founder of Rome, and conveyed the notion that he was the second founder, as well as an almost divine being, supreme in authority during his sojourn on earth.

The wreaths of bay leaves are a sign of victory, and the civic crown, a wreath of oak leaves, had always been given for conspicuous bravery in saving the life of a fellow citizen; Dio makes it clear (LIII, 16, 4) that it was awarded to Augustus for 'saving the citizens', a theme echoed in literature and on coins inscribed *ob cives servatos*, 'for saving the citizens', with an accompanying representation of the crown and oak leaves. Cf. the next section and 3,1 n. The golden shield was dedicated in the Senate House (*Curia*) close to the altar of Victory, and celebrated Augustus' virtues. The first of these, *virtus*, we render 'courage', for lack of an exact equivalent; it is more than courage, rather the quality that enables a man to perform great services, especially in war, for his state (cf. D. C. Earl, *Political Thought of Sallust*, chapters II and III); it underlies all Augustus' services to Rome. Clemency is paraded in 3,1–2 and symbolized, along with *virtus*, in the civic crown (*supra*). Justice is exemplified in 26,3, and piety in the retribution he exacted from his father's murderers (2), in his returning statues stolen from temples (24) and in the restoration of the temples in 28 BC (20,4). The reader is expected to see that a man whose virtues were so outstanding that they received this signal recognition from the senate and people was plainly worthy of the exceptional authority that he continued to enjoy in the state.

34,3. We translate *quŏque*, not *quōque*. If the latter be read, then Augustus is saying that he had no more power than others whom he had as colleagues in a magistracy, and is indicating his magnanimity in allowing any one to share office with him; this seems unlikely. If *quŏque* be read, however, there is a difficulty. Most naturally the words would mean that he had colleagues in more than one kind of magistracy. But after 27 Augustus held, strictly, no magistracy except the consulship, and after 23 he was, except in two years, technically a proconsul, i.e. not a magistrate, but a promagistrate. Similarly, the fact that he held tribunician power did not make him a holder of the office, or magistracy, of the tribunate. Hence, though he took colleagues in the tribunician power, they were not his colleagues in a magistracy. He also allowed Agrippa and Tiberius to hold *imperium*, like his own proconsular or (in our view) consular *imperium*; but as holders of such *imperium*, they were no more magistrates than he was himself; moreover, there is some doubt whether their *imperium* at all times was co-extensive with his own; if he was entitled to exercise it in Italy, and they were not, they did not possess as much legal power as he did. None the less, some ordinary readers at Rome may have understood Augustus' statement to refer to the position of Agrippa and Tiberius, although he should have meant that he held no more legal power *as consul* than those who were his colleagues in each of the consulships he held from 27 onwards. This differentiates his position as consul after the settlement of January 27 from that which he had occupied up to 28, when he had arrogated to himself a formal superiority over his colleagues (34,1 n.). His statement is only a half-truth; though his colleagues from 27 evidently enjoyed formal equality with him in Rome as consuls, they were not his equals even in legal power, when we take into account both the vast province he governed and, in regard to his consulships in 5 and 2 BC, the tribunician power that he also possessed at least from 23 BC.

The division of power between equal colleagues was an important principle of the Republic. When the monarchy fell, in Tacitus' words (*Ann.* I, 1), 'Lucius Brutus established freedom and the consulate', i.e. an office in which the royal power was divided. Augustus here claims that he respected this Republican principle of collegiality. But the claim has so little relevance to his position after 23 that it is plausible to hold that this sentence was originally written in the earliest draft of the *Res Gestae*, perhaps by 23 (cf. p. 6), with reference to the years in which his annual tenure of the consulship was the legal basis of his power; as it had not ceased to be true in some sense thereafter, and still created a desirable impression that Augustus had been careful of constitutional proprieties, he was probably content to leave it unchanged in later drafts.

He contrasts his legal power (*potestas*) with his influence (*auctoritas*), cf. Cic., *in Pisonem*, 8; 'Quintus Metellus, consul elect . . . as a private citizen vetoed' the action of a tribune, and 'what he could not yet achieve through power (*potestate*) he obtained through influence (*auctoritate*)'; see further pp. 84f. In the Republic the leading citizens (*principes*) had *auctoritas*, as this text shows; Augustus, as the leading citizen (*princeps*) *par excellence* claims to have had more than any other man, as the proper result of his pre-eminent services to Rome. It need hardly be said that he is not implying that he lacked such *auctoritas* before 27. But previously he had enjoyed autocratic *power*; he qualifies the statement that after 27 he lacked such power by claiming that he still excelled others in influence. There is no need to make this statement the keystone of an account of Augustus' constitutional position after 27; his influence is indeed important, but he also retained extensive legal powers by which he could justify his actions.

35. For more details of this honour, see Suet. *Aug.* 58. The title of 'parent of his fatherland' had been bestowed unofficially on Cicero after he suppressed the Catilinarian conspiracy, and officially on Caesar, if Dio (XLIV, 4, 4) and Suetonius (*Caesar* 85) are right. About 29 BC Horace had prayed that Augustus might wish to defer his return to Heaven and to be called 'father and chief citizen' (*pater atque princeps*) below (*Odes* I, 2, 45ff.). Livy V, 49, 7 represents Camillus, who in legend saved Rome from the Gauls, as a second Romulus and as 'parent of his fatherland'; the name 'Augustus' conveyed a similar suggestion about its holder (34,2 n.). The conception that Augustus was father of his country is also foreshadowed in the cult of the Genius of Augustus (for which see Horace, *Ep.* II, 1, 15f.; L. R. Taylor, *Divinity of the Roman Emperor*, pp. 151f. and chapter VII). The Genius, the mysterious power (*numen*) residing in the head of the household, in primitive times the power by which his procreative ability could be explained, had always been an object of cult within the family; to make the Genius of Augustus an object of public cult implied that he stood in the same relation to Rome as the father did to his own household; see further, Warde Fowler, *Roman Ideas of Deity*, pp. 17ff., or *Religious Experience of the Roman People*, pp. 74ff. The cult had become official in 14/3 BC. The unanimity with which this new transcendent honour was granted to Augustus makes it a fitting climax to his memorial, recorded with due ceremony.

Appendix. This is a summary not written by Augustus of his expenses on public objects. The author gives a total in section 1 in *denarii*, not sesterces[1]; this is higher than the sum of individual items as stated by Augustus; but Augustus probably chose to mention only the more notable instances of his generosity, and the summarizer may have included gifts omitted by Augustus, merely because he had brought his list up to date (15 n.). As the addition of the summary weakens the effect of Augustus' peroration, it can hardly have formed part of the monument at Rome.

Why was it appended at Ancyra? In 4 we have a reference to his liberality to towns (*oppida*), and the Greek version makes it explicit that

---

[1] Augustus only once uses the term *denarii* (15,4); 1 *denarius* = 4 sesterces.

provincial towns are included. For such liberality, cf. Dio LIV, 30, 3;
Suet., *Aug.* 47; *Tib.* 8. Augustus himself did not allude to it; the point
of 24,1 is quite different, see note *ad loc.* Perhaps, then, the author of the
Appendix was more concerned with provincial readers than Augustus
himself had been. Yet he too dwells otherwise only on his benefactions to
the state, the soldiers, the city and inhabitants of Rome, and to senators
and 'friends', i.e. highly-placed Romans; for these last benefactions see,
e.g. Suet., *Aug.* 41; Dio LIII, 2, 1f.; LIV, 17, 3. All this was of little
interest to provincials such as the Galatians. The purpose of the Appendix
remains an enigma.

ADDENDA TO NOTES

6,2.   In 1970 L. Koenen published a fragment of a Greek papyrus
which is clearly translated from a funeral oration pronounced by Augustus
on Agrippa (see now for a discussion in English, E. W. Gray, *Zeitschrift
für Papyrologie und Epigraphik* VI, 1970, 227 ff.). This states: 'The
tribunician power was conferred on you [i.e. Agrippa] for five years in
accordance with a decree of the senate in the consulship of the Lentuli
[18 BC] and again for another Olympiad [i.e. for five more years] in that
of Tiberius Nero and Quinctilius Varus, your sons-in-law [13 BC], and it
was ratified by law that to whatsoever provinces [*hyparcheias*, an unusual
Greek rendering] the common interests of the Romans [or 'the Roman
state'] might draw you, no one in those provinces should have greater
power than you . . .' Apart from attesting for the first time that Varus,
governor of Syria 6–4 BC, and legate on the Rhine, AD 7–9, where he and
his army were destroyed by the Germans, was married to an otherwise
unknown Vipsania, daughter of Agrippa, this seems to show (i) that
Agrippa's *imperium* was restricted to provinces he actually visited, like
that of C. Cassius in the east in 43 BC (Cicero, *Philippics* XI, 30) and of
Germanicus beyond the Adriatic in AD 17 (Tacitus, *Annals* II, 43); (ii)
that, unlike that of Cassius and Germanicus, it was not superior but only
equal to that of provincial governors; (iii) that this grant was made in
13 BC; hence any earlier grant of *imperium* to Agrippa must have been
less extensive, presumably restricted to named provinces. However,
though this is the natural interpretation, it *may* be held that the date in
the papyrus refers only to the grant of tribunician power, that the
recorded grant of *imperium* was earlier than 13 BC, and that Augustus
may have gone on to mention that Agrippa's *imperium* was made *maius*
in 13 BC; this is not very plausible, but it is the only way to save Dio's
statement (LIV, 28,1) that in 13 BC he received greater power than each
governor had in his province.

26,2. Augustus personally administered Gaul and Spain in 27–24 and 16–13. In Gaul there was little trouble, but Velleius II, 90 justly stresses his success in completing the pacification of Spain, where some of the peoples had not been fully subdued in nearly two centuries of Roman occupation; see also EJ 42. As to Germany, if 'Germaniam' can be taken in apposition to 'provincias', then Augustus here claims that the land between Rhine and Elbe had been made a province, and our comment is mistaken. But more probably he is contrasting Germany with the existing Gallic and Spanish provinces. However, in any event he may deliberately have chosen to ignore Varus' defeat, and it may be imprudent to infer from his allusion to Germany that he had not fully revised the *Res Gestae* after AD 9.

26,4. See also Velleius II, 106; Pliny, *Natural History* II, 167; Strabo VII, 2,1. Mention of the Cimbri would have recalled the grave danger that Cimbric incursions presented to Italy itself at the end of the second century.

28. In Augustus' time there were also several colonies in Illyricum, which he ignores either because they had been founded by Caesar or because they were not settled by soldiers. He also passes over colonies he founded for soldiers in Mauretania, a client kingdom, probably because they came under the jurisdiction of the Roman governors of Africa or Baetica and could be regarded as belonging to those provinces.

APPENDIX

SOME ROMAN CONSTITUTIONAL TERMS

THE most general term in Latin denoting official legal power is *potestas*. All magistrates, including those possessed of *imperium*, had *potestas*. But the legal power of some magistrates, e.g. the tribunes (cf. p. 11), was limited to the performance of certain defined actions. By contrast *imperium* is a discretionary power to do what the interest of the state requires; except in so far as the holder of *imperium* may be specifically forbidden to do certain things, he is free to do what he thinks fit. In particular, military command and jurisdiction in serious cases belong only to holders of *imperium*. Their powers, however, cannot be exhaustively enumerated, as the powers of a tribune can.

In the Republic *imperium* could be limited in two ways, by laws which forbade the holder to do certain things, e.g. to put a citizen to death arbitrarily, and by the veto of magistrates with equal or higher power. All ten tribunes had negatively and within the city of Rome, but not outside it, such a higher power against the consuls and praetors, who held *imperium*, and could (with certain exceptions) veto their acts. Each consul had equal power with his colleague and consequently the right to obstruct him. The consuls had *imperium* superior to the praetors (*imperium maius*) and could overrule them, though they seldom did.

The consuls and praetors were elected for a year, but it became common in the Republic to entrust them with provinces after their year of office had expired; they were then proconsuls or propraetors, which means that they were as good as consuls or praetors. This was not quite true, since such promagistrates forfeited their *imperium* if they came inside the *pomerium*, the old sacred boundary of the city of Rome. Of course they could not perform the functions of consuls and praetors as magistrates within the city of Rome. Moreover, normally they did not *exercise imperium* within Italy during the late Republic. But in their own provinces they could exercise *imperium* to the full, unimpeded by a veto, since they had no colleagues there, and hardly checked by laws circumscribing their powers; they were virtually absolute. Perhaps a consul technically had superior power (*imperium maius*) as against a proconsul, but it was at most rare for a consul to send instructions to a proconsul in a province. It seems clear, however, that between 27 and 23 Augustus did avail himself of his formal superiority as consul to give orders to proconsuls in senatorial provinces (cf. 24,1n). His own provinces he governed by deputies with praetorian *imperium* (*legati pro praetore*) or (as in Egypt) by equestrian prefects (who also had *imperium*); they were subordinate to him, since he was either consul or after 23 had *imperium* as a proconsul and was thereby superior to propraetors.

Mommsen indeed held that since the time of Sulla consuls and praetors, as such, were debarred from governing or interfering in provinces which were reserved to proconsuls and propraetors, and consequently that when Augustus 'restored the Republic' in 27, although he was consul at the time, he needed a grant of proconsular *imperium* to govern his provinces. Mommsen's theory that Sulla made it a legal or conventional rule (which Augustus would have observed) that a consul as such could not govern a province has, however, been refuted by J. P. V. D. Balsdon (*JRS* (1939), 57ff.). Further, the adjective 'proconsular' is not found in the Republic, and Cicero describes the *imperium* of promagistrates governing provinces as consular (*pro Flac*. 85; *in Pis*. 38; 55); it would therefore have been most un-republican and almost nonsensical to say that Augustus had proconsular *imperium* when he was consul. Mommsen's theory, which has been generally repeated, must be rejected. We should suppose that in 27 Augustus was voted certain provinces for ten years (the term was later renewed for periods of five or ten years until his death), which he governed as consul until 23, and thereafter as proconsul. It was in accordance with Republican practice that his *imperium* was automatically continued in 23, when he laid the consulship down, since he already had a province in which to exercise it.

If Cicero's usage was still followed, the *imperium* of Augustus would still have been described as consular even after 23, although it would have been unconventional for him to use it in Italy, just as if he were still consul and not proconsul. What happened in 19 was perhaps that then his right was acknowledged to exercise his consular power for all purposes even in Rome and Italy; cf pp. 13–14. In fact his pre-eminent *auctoritas* enabled him to exercise it in various ways which even a consul in the late Republic would not normally have ventured on.

Potestas stands in contrast to *auctoritas*. This word is derived from *auctor*, a term which denotes, for instance, the guarantor of the validity of a sale, or of the validity of the legal acts of a minor, or the mover or backer of a proposal. *Auctoritas* means the influence or prestige which ensures that one's views are accepted. In the Republic it belonged pre-eminently to the senate. In theory the senate was only the advisory council of the magistrates; in practice the magistrates were expected to do what it advised, though it never gave instructions but only said that they should do something 'if they saw fit'. *Auctoritas* also belonged to leading senators, men who had held the highest offices (*principes*). In a passage describing German chiefs but redolent of Roman ideas, Tacitus says 'that they were listened to in proportion to their age, their nobility, their military reputation and their eloquence, more from the influence they had to persuade than from their legal power to command' (*auctoritate suadendi magis quam iubendi potestate*) (*Germania* 11). With *potestas* a man gives orders that must be obeyed, with *auctoritas* he makes suggestions that will be followed. Yet, though contrasted, the ideas are linked. Cicero claimed that he had as much *auctoritas* as the people had vested in him by electing him to offices (*de imperio Cn. Pompeii* 2). The holder of *imperium* has *auctoritas* as such, though he will not necessarily lose it when he goes out of office.

Augustus, the *princeps par excellence*, claimed to be supreme in *auctoritas* (34,3 n.). It has been held that much of his control of the state can be explained in this way. It is important to note, however, that he had military command and jurisdiction only in virtue of his *imperium*. None the less, his pre-eminent *auctoritas* may have enabled him to exercise *imperium* in ways which no ordinary holder of the same legal powers would have dared to do. Moreover he might have preferred to use *auctoritas*, when he could have used *imperium*, because he wanted to carry public opinion with him, persuading rather than commanding, and to ensure the genuine co-operation of men in high places, who might have resented commands and yet have been ready to take advice. Dio says that in 23 he was granted superior *imperium* to other proconsuls. This meant that he could give them instructions. We sometimes find that he or Tiberius did so (EJ, 312 and 291 for instructions to proconsuls in Asia and Africa). But when he intervened in the senatorial province of Cyrenaica, he said that the proconsuls would act 'rightly and fittingly' if they adopted certain reforms in jurisdiction which he proposed (EJ, 311, I); this was the kind of language the senate employed in making recommendations to magistrates. It was tactful, but it does not imply that Augustus had not the right to give orders. At the very same time he did give orders to the provincials in Cyrenaica without reference to the proconsuls (EJ, 311, III). There is no reason to doubt Dio's statement on his power. Moreover, Augustus' *auctoritas*, founded on his high birth, great achievements and unexampled accumulation of offices and legal powers, was not inherited by all his successors. Tiberius could have claimed the same pre-eminence, but not Caligula, Claudius or Nero. Their control was founded on their legal powers and command of the army, yet they had no more legal powers than Augustus, and there had been no vital change in the military balance; from Gaius the emperors commanded the whole army, but even in AD 14 only the African legion was outside Augustus' command. It can therefore be seen that supreme *auctoritas* was not the basis of the Principate, though it assisted Augustus to found a system which lesser men could work.

CHRONOLOGICAL TABLE

BC

63	23 Sept.	Birth of Augustus, then called C. Octavius.
44	15 March	Assassination of Julius Caesar.
		C. Octavius, adopted by Caesar's will becomes C. Iulius Caesar.
	Summer	Octavian in Rome quarrels with Antony.
	October	He raises an army against Antony (*RG* 1).
43	January	He is given *imperium* by the senate (*RG* 1).
	April	Defeat of Antony at Mutina.
	August	Octavian marches on Rome and is elected to his first consulship (*RG* 1).
	Autumn	Formation of triumvirate. Proscriptions.
42		Philippi campaign. Battles fought in October and November (*RG* 2).
41		While Antony is in the east, Octavian organizes distribution of lands to veterans; outbreak of war with the consul, Lucius Antonius.
		Parthians overrun large parts of Asia.
40	February	Surrender of Lucius Antonius at Perusia.
		Octavian in control of all Italy.
	Autumn	Reconciliation of Octavian and Antony at the pact of Brundisium.
39		Short-lived pact between the triumvirs and Sextus Pompey at Misenum.
39–8		Parthians driven out of Roman territory by Antony's generals.
38–7		Octavian at war with Sextus Pompey.
36		Octavian eliminates Sextus Pompey and Lepidus. Antony's Parthian disaster.
35–4		Octavian's victorious Illyrian campaigns.
34		Antony annexes Armenia.
33–2		Antony and Octavian prepare for war with each other. The triumvirate expires at the end of one of these years.
32		The oath taken to Octavian in Italy (*RG* 25). War declared against Cleopatra.
31–23		Octavian consul each year.

BC

31	Sept.	Battle of Actium.
30		Death of Antony and Cleopatra. Egypt annexed.
30–27		Period of Octavian's greatest munificence. Great discharge of veterans.
29		Closure of temple of Janus. Augustus' triple triumph (Dalmatia, Actium, Egypt) (*RG* 4).
28		The first Augustan census.
28–7		'Restoration of the Republic', culminating in the
27	16 Jan.	conferment on Octavian of the name Augustus.
27–24		Augustus in Spain and Gaul.
23		Augustus surrenders the consulship and receives other powers in compensation; he counts his tribunician power from this year.
		Death of Marcellus, Augustus' son-in-law and probably intended heir.
22		Augustus refuses dictatorship and perpetual consulship.
22–19		Augustus in the East.
21		Agrippa married to Augustus' daughter, Julia.
20		Settlement with Armenia and Parthia.
19		Augustus' return to Rome. (He may now have received new powers giving him more legal power in Rome and Italy.)
18		Agrippa becomes his colleague in tribunician power (and in *imperium*). 'Moral' legislation (*RG* 6).
17		Augustus adopts Gaius and Lucius Caesar, Agrippa's sons by Julia.
		Secular Games.
16–13		Augustus in Gaul, Agrippa in the East.
16		Beginning of the great conquests in the north, in which Augustus' stepsons, Tiberius and Drusus, play leading parts.
13		Agrippa's tribunician power renewed.
13–12		Death of Lepidus; Augustus becomes *pontifex maximus* (*RG* 10).
12		Death of Agrippa.
9		Death of Augustus' younger stepson, Drusus.
6		Tiberius made Augustus' colleague in tribunician power, but then retires to Rhodes.
5		Gaius Caesar introduced to public life.
2		Lucius Caesar introduced to public life.
1		Tiberius' tribunician power expires.

AD		
1–4		Gaius Caesar in the East.
2		Tiberius returns from quasi-exile.
		Death of Lucius Caesar.
4		Death of Gaius Caesar. Augustus adopts Tiberius and makes him partner in tribunician power (renewed in 13).
6		Revolt in Pannonia and Dalmatia puts an end to Roman expansion northwards.
9		As soon as this revolt is over, Arminius in Germany destroys Varus' legions.
14	19 Aug.	Death of Augustus.

INDEX

THIS is a select index of allusions in the introduction, notes and appendix to the main topics and to persons on whom some information is given.